CITY OF JOY

CITY OF JOY

✤ THE ILLUSTRATED STORY OF THE FILM ✤

Roland Joffé, Mark Medoff, and Jake Eberts

Afterword by Dominique Lapierre

Photographs by David Appleby
and other contributors

Edited by Diana Landau

A NEWMARKET PICTORIAL MOVIEBOOK

Newmarket Press · New York

Compilation and original text copyright © 1992 by Newmarket Press
Screenplay by Mark Medoff copyright © 1991 by Lightmotive, Ltd. and
    Allied Filmmakers, N.V.
Introduction copyright © 1992 by Roland Joffé
Producer's Journal copyright © 1992 by Jake Eberts
Screenwriter's Note copyright © 1992 by Mark Medoff
Afterword copyright © 1992 by Dominique Lapierre
Photographs by David Appleby, Stephen F. Morley, Dirck Halstead,
    and *City of Joy* Art Department copyright © 1991 by Lightmotive,
    Ltd. and Allied Filmmakers, N.V.
All other photographs copyrighted by the photographer credited.

Credits and acknowledgments of permission for illustrations and text
    reprinted from other works will be found on page 157. All photo-
    graphs not otherwise credited are by David Appleby.

Features about the cast, crew, and filmmaking process are adapted
    from interviews and production notes by Ann Tasker, with original
    research added.

This book published simultaneously in the United States of America
    and in Canada.

92 93 94   10 9 8 7 6 5 4 3 2 1

Library of Congress Cataloging-in-Publication Data

Joffé, Roland, 1945-
    City of Joy: the illustrated story of the film / Roland Joffé,
    Mark Medoff, Jake Eberts; afterword by Dominique Lapierre.
        p.   cm.
    ISBN 1-55704-124-5 (hc) — ISBN 1-55704-125-3 (pb)
    1. City of Joy (Motion picture). I. Medoff, Mark Howard.
    II. Eberts, Jake. III. Title.
    PN1997.C5155J64   1992
    791.43'72—dc20   92-1163
                                            CIP

Quantity Purchases
Companies, professional groups, clubs, and other organizations may
qualify for special terms when ordering quantities of this title. For
information, write: Special Sales, Newmarket Press, 18 East 48th
Street, New York, N.Y. 10017, or call (212) 832-3575.

Editorial, design, and production services by Walking Stick Press,
    San Francisco: Diana Landau, editor; Linda Herman, book design;
    Robert Cornish, design associate.

Newmarket Productions staff: Esther Margolis, director; Keith Hollaman,
    editor; Walter Friedman, production ; Susan Rosalsky, permissions;
    Anna Shah, administration.

Manufactured in the United States of America

First Edition

Other Newmarket Pictorial Moviebooks include:
Dances With Wolves: The Illustrated Story of the Epic Film
Far and Away: The Illustrated Story of a Journey from Ireland to America
The Inner Circle: An Inside View of Soviet Life Under Stalin
Gandhi: A Pictorial Biography

Cover photographs by David Appleby and Dirck Halstead.

❖ Contents ❖

❖ Calcutta: The Quality of the Struggle ❖

by Roland Joffé

Roland Joffé directs a scene on a Calcutta street.

This is a crossroads. Five streets converge on this city square . . . well, more of a triangle. One street, wider than the others and fitting into them like a handle into a broom, is blocked by a camera crane and two electrical generator trucks bearing the proud emblem "Lee Electrics, Shepperton Studios, England." It's also blocked by a huge articulated crane capable of spraying filtered artificial rain over everything in front of its snout. Before it, gathered in lightly defensive order, is a camera crew of some hundred assorted souls: Indian, English, Irish, Scottish, French, American, Italian. It seems that a film is about to start shooting . . . or maybe not.

In the center of the triangle stands a motley and slightly embarrassed mob. Red banners wave in the damp air; the hammer and sickle sway on a red cloth slung between two poles. The crowd is chanting. I know the words by heart. Loosely translated from Bengali, they have become our anthem—"City of Joy, go home." After a quick glance at my watch, I rustle up a smile and a wave for the brood of photographers who materialize with uncanny accuracy every time we have one of these little dramas. Time for a cup of tea. The negotiations will probably last an hour yet, then the leaders of the moblet, imperialist dollars held tight in their fists, will head off into the back streets, honor satisfied.

I sit down near the camera, take a slug of lukewarm tea. This is almost the last week of filming. I realize with a pang just how much I'm going to miss all this fervor; how much I'm going to miss Calcutta. I have a moment to let my mind drift. . . .

"But going there to make a movie! That's naive, bloody naive, and you know it." This from a friend, a foreign correspondent

Bathing in the Hooghly River, Calcutta, 1890's. Photo by Johnston and Hoffman.

of immaculate reputation, at the Chelsea Arts Club in London. I ask why and he rolls his eyes, then runs through a quick list of those who have suffered from Calcutta's collective ire, from Louis Malle to Günther Grass.

Naive or not, a few weeks later I step off a Thai jet into the humid embrace of West Bengal.

The drive from the airport is unexpectedly pastoral. Flame trees shade the road in between a seemingly endless succession of small villages. Mud houses, cows, luminous colored saris managing somehow to dry in the moist air. Children are everywhere, bright, smiling, curious.

The houses become smaller, made of scraps of wood, cloth, old billboards. These aren't villages but the homes of refugees—some from the rigor of the countryside, some left over from from the Partition of 1948 or the war in Bangladesh. Then, abruptly, I find myself in the city. Unlike some cities, Calcutta does not float in a sea of shantytowns; it has embraced its refugees, or they it. They do not wait on its outskirts but live in it, on its pavements, wherever there is a rare open space.

The historic capital of the British Raj, Calcutta was once extremely rich. Now it is a fecund, intricate maze of streets dotted with the dumpy and decaying presences of myriad colonial palaces. Once magnificent, fantastic essays in brick and marble, now these massive structures—like trees in the Amazo-

This white-haired man, a rickshaw puller, is only 45 years old. He proudly holds his baby son, his assurance that someone will care for him in his old age and lead his cremation ceremony according to Hindu rites. Photo by Dominique Lapierre.

nian jungle—are barely discernible beneath the weight of countless smaller dwellings. Eleven million souls inhabit this city, whose surface area is not much bigger than Manhattan. The city is splitting open with what is both its wealth and its burden—its teeming, milling crowds, all needing to be fed, watered, sheltered, succored. More jammed than New York's subways at rush hour, people and traffic boil through the streets, maniacally purposeful.

It is easy to get accustomed to the city—many Calcuttans tell me they have learned to look without seeing—but that first visceral shock is difficult to forget. It forces a confrontation with our own humanity that is disturbing, but also unexpectedly energizing.

The images of Calcutta are striking and restless, constantly shifting in meaning. A small family has made a home on the street, underneath a huge, blackened flyover (a roadway overpass). All they possess could easily be packed into a tote bag. The father is dandling a baby on his bony knees, massaging its neck as the child stares up at him and gurgles. Look once, and this image of poverty hurts; look again, and the love passing from father to son is palpable, heartwarming, heroic under the circumstances. The mother, almost invisible, is sorting garbage in the background while the father holds the child; the meaning shifts again. You can take your choice: all three interpretations are valid, and probably several more. To select only one at the expense of others, as Western visitors often do, is to miss the point.

Behind the Grand Hotel, a well-preserved relic of Calcutta's colonial grandeur, is a pitch worked by a couple of beggars. One is deposited each day from a small cart onto a square of pavement. Literally deposited; the man's limbs were broken at birth and reset so that he resembles a human knot. The sight is grotesque, appalling, stomach-churning . . . until you look into his eyes. Their penetrating gaze asks for your money but not your pity. What I think it tells me is this: "I am not my circumstances. It is outrageous that any person has to live in this way. For this I ask help. But I also surmount my circumstances. I am a human knot; I am also a heroic knot, and for this I demand respect."

About eight or ten miles from Calcutta's center is one of Mother Teresa's self-help centers for lepers, a simple collection of houses and workshops radiating out from the railway track. I am charmed by the generous smile of the young Indian priest showing me around. But my stomach is in knots, and I have to steel myself to drink the cup of sweet tea he proffers. I've never

> "About ninety miles inland the head of the Bay of Bengal, the Hooghly [River], which generally runs from north to south, loops in a semicircular bend toward the west, creating a bulge of land on the eastern bank. This bulge marks the uppermost point of the river which is navigable by ocean-going ships, and it was around this point that the European traders —Portuguese, Dutch, French, and British, in that order—who sailed up the river in the sixteenth and seventeenth centuries, founded their settlements. The British settlement, which was established on the bulge in 1690 by Job Charnock, of the East India Company, and was called Calcutta, grew into the capital of British India. . . ."
>
> Ved Mehta,
> *A Portrait of India*

heard of anyone catching leprosy through tea, but my imagination is beginning to run riot.

We walk through a workshop where about forty women work at looms, many operating the shuttles with fingerless hands. The brother stops to tell one woman that her weaving is not up to par. To me it seems a little hard that he had made so little allowance for her handicap. But the rebuke earns a shy smile. In making no allowances, the young man treated the woman as an equal, not a victim. As we crunch across the gravel between the tracks, I put this to the priest. "Certainly, compassion may conceal contempt," he says. "It makes me feel good, superior even, but my pity is an intolerable burden to its object. Extending help to an equal makes us both feel valued."

Some years ago the local mafia decided that this little colony—which received modest amounts of aid, dried milk, foodstuffs, and the like—might be a source of profit. They announced the imposition of a "tax" on the aid; after some discussion, the monks and lepers refused to pay it. The gangsters responded by sealing off the colony, kidnapping one of the monks, and threatening to send him back piece by piece unless they capitulated. The local police vanished; there was no escape and no telephone; all were at their wits' end.

Roland Joffé and the film crew prepare to shoot a scene of striking rickshaw workers.

> "Calcutta is the youngest of all the big modern cities on the globe. Manhattan was founded eighty-one years before Job Charnock pitched his tents on the banks of the river Hooghly . . . , and Maisonneuve created Montreal half a century earlier.
>
> "No such place called Calcutta, or indeed a country by the name of India, existed before the British arrived. They created both entities. But the ferment, the chaos, the grinding, putrefying, head-long rush into the suspended animation of total infirmity, which everyone predicts, but which, miraculously, never seems to happen, is the result of an old civilization confronting the vital exuberant arrogance of a newer one. Poised in tableaux, teeth gnashing in fierce acrimony, . . . the city survives—continues to exist."
>
> Sasthi Brata,
> *India: Labyrinths in Lotus Land*

All but one elderly, blind leper. Familiar with his dark world, he managed to make his way out of the colony at night, evading the murderous guards posted around it, climb on a train, and get to Calcutta. Once there, he got to Mother Teresa's convent and raised the alarm, and hence the siege. I'm introduced to this man, whose name is Das. He sits on his little wooden bed, straight-backed, hands bandaged, seeing nothing through his eyes. I shake his hand. . . .

Calcutta has more than one red-light district. This one is favored mainly by out-of-towners. Like so many streets near the city center, this is a maze of old palaces, subdivided and redivided again. Calcutta is a hymn to the impermanence of things, though part of its charm is its unfazed acceptance of this fact. Camus would have loved this city with its Sisyphean message about the futility and dignity of human effort.

Part of one such grand old house is now a small hotel catering to poor Indians and poorer Westerners. The man I have come to see occupies a tiny space that should be a cupboard but advertises itself as a room. Sitting on the bed is Dr. Jack Preger, one of a handful of Western doctors and nurses who have chosen to live and work in Calcutta. A pale, drawn Irish Jew, sometime past converted to Catholicism, he radiates nervous energy and a manic sense of humor. Dr. Jack runs a street clinic, managing with laughably small resources to provide care and medicine to as many as 800 souls. He's a maverick, deeply unappealing to the notoriously self-opinionated Indian bureaucracy, so he works virtually unsupported.

He takes me through a tale of horrors, of forgotten children and unnoticed deaths, prostitution, illness, malnutrition, wife-burning and beating—Dante's inferno. But it is his manner of telling that strikes me: a matter-of-fact acceptance that this is his world to cope with. More, he's committed to it. He points out that the big difference between him and his clients is that he can leave whenever he wants. But that's not quite true. He can't leave, because the humanity of the place has worked its alchemy on his system. He's giving, he's in the struggle, he's connected, he has a purpose, and he's alive. He looks at me across the narrow, sweaty room and asks how anyone could want more. He's in love with the city, though it turns its official back on him. In our more pristine society, this attitude would and did qualify him as an oddball. Here, he makes sense, and makes the rest of us losers.

Sometime later I go to visit one of Calcutta's more impressive cultural icons, the film director Satyajit Ray. Tropical nights fall early, and this one catches us mid-interview. Ray sits in a tall wing chair, his back to the failing light. I sit rather uncomfortably in a much lower chair to his left, looking up at him. It may be an effect of the light, but Ray's aristocratic and momentarily expressionless visage seems carved out of stone, like the Hindu gods I have seen in a temple near Bombay.

Ray has just announced that only a Calcuttan, or at least an Indian, could make a film about Calcutta. Further, it is quite impossible, he says, for a low-caste Indian farmer to form any kind of relationship with a European. This was precisely the kind of thing I came to Calcutta to research, but my conclusions were different from Ray's. Only that morning I'd interviewed a young volunteer of Dr. Jack's who had formed a very close relationship with a patient, and had heard similar stories from other volunteers. I tell this to Ray, who nods dismissively and then says, "Also your film is all about lepers. I see no lepers on the streets of the city." This is a bit of a stunner. After a pause, he adds, "Maybe I don't get around as much as I did."

Then a long silence falls. I think of the attacks on Louis Malle, on Günther Grass. Is this my first encounter with Bengali *amour propre?* Grass, in his book on the city, describes daily living in Calcutta as an exercise in denial. He's right in a way. Calcutta assaults the senses, and some of what it offers has to be mentally filtered out. Clearly, bourgeois Calcuttans don't take kindly to Europeans, strangers, puncturing their protective mechanisms. Making a film here is going to require balancing on a tightrope suspended over a Niagara Falls of complex emotions.

Later, after all our pleasantries have been exchanged, Ray says ominously, "You won't be able to shoot on the streets of Calcutta, you know. It can't be done. Even I would have extreme difficulty." As I groped down the murky stairwell, it seems pretty clear to me that Ray doesn't much want the film to be made. The question is, why not?

That question was answered in part a couple of days earlier, in the office of a very savvy, very urbane senior minister in the Marxist government of West Bengal. In the cultivated, nasal English of an Oxford professor he explains that our film will not give a "true" picture of the city. The problem seems to be that it is a film about poor people, about the underbelly of a city, with a cast that includes prostitutes, mafia, con men—the usual denizens of any metropolis, but not, in official eyes at least, of Calcutta. "It would," he pronounces with a light smile, "insult the cultural heritage of the Bengali people."

My mind crowds with images: the human knot, the destitute queuing up outside the street clinic, a family making life

Indian film director Satyajit Ray, photographed in 1963 by Sunil Janah.

"I love Calcutta, I have lived here all my life. The best of whatever is being done in the arts in India is being done here. There is great intellectual vitality. . . . Only film-making has not attracted many intellectuals, yet from a film-maker's point of view no city could be better. . . ."

Satyajit Ray

under a blackened flyover, the heroic Mr. Das, and all the other ignored souls who give this city its inimitable spirit. I wonder whether this is a matter of understandable civic pride, or something deeper. It is plain that we are dealing not with questions of reality here, but of perception; questions of image, particularly in relation to the admired and despised West. As the minister continues speaking, I gather that he could digest, as easily as he does the moist biscuits on his plate, our awkward desire to film in this city, if we were here to make some affectionate romance of the Raj. His worry, understandable in the circumstances, is that we are depicting not what was, but what is.

A much-conquered people throughout their history, the Indians have coped with invasions partly through passivity, partly through accommodation, or manipulation, or patient absorption. This enabled them to cushion the impact of despotism, imposed language, and squeezing taxation. Eventually invader and invaded settled into a kind of seamless alliance, which nevertheless concealed great personal and social tension.

These tensions called into effect a simple, potent human response to powerlessness, to the unendurable: denial. India has refined this instinctual response into something close to an art form. The national character exhibits intense pride laminated to a deeply conflicted core, an avoidance of self-analysis, a drive to transfer internal anxieties to some suitably external cause. If a nation can be said to have a collective personality, then the passive-aggressive is a binding strand in the personality of the Indian subcontinent.

If Calcutta is a city of decaying palaces, it is also a city of apartments—some of nineteenth-century spaciousness, others, perpendicular and concrete, the result of a surge of building that began in the late 'fifties. I'm sitting in one of the latter, the home of Sunil Gangopadhayay. One of Bengal's most observant writers and sometime screenwriter for Satyajit Ray, Sunil is acting as an in-depth consultant on our screenplay. This lively and witty man has been guiding me through the labyrinthine psychological and political byways of the city.

Sunil displays none of the rhetorical suspicion, the ideological rigidity I'd encountered in some of the city's other intellectuals. I tell him that word has been put out that I am "virulently anti-Marxist," and that the party faithful have been advised to lock their mental doors against my imperialist wiles. Sunil doesn't say anything, but I know he's come under pressure too. He shrugs it off, driven by his inner clarity. Sunil doesn't submit to any party line. He is fascinated by Calcutta and loves it, warts and all. I stop my lament. A voice calls outside the window; somewhere a love song weaves through the crowded air. Not for the first or last time, Sunil and I go over the script, refining, scrutinizing, finding a voice, searching out a detailed life for Hasari Pal, rickshaw puller.

It's said that the sisters who spin our fate are blind, but I'm convinced that sometimes they cheat; there are seeing eyes under the blindfold. Several years after my first long trip to India, I was in London editing *The Mission* and went to a Christmas service at Westminster Abbey. Afterwards, warming up with a glass of punch at the fine old school across the way, I find myself in conversation with the headmaster's wife. The talk turns to India, and she says, "I happen to be proofreading something that might interest you." What she was reading was the proof of an English translation of a book by the French author Dominique Lapierre. Two days later I was reading the manuscript. And there it was, amidst a cornucopia of detail: the story of Hasari Pal—father, farmer, rickshaw puller. I could barely sleep that night. A day or so later, I dropped by to see Jake Eberts, who was busy trying to patch together his old company, Goldcrest Films. Jake asked what I wanted to do next. . . .

So, some four years after that question, here I was in a Calcutta taxi, threading through the graceful crowds of an evening market, sucking in the noise, the color, the contradictions, the paranoias that make up the life of this city. Trying to catch this energy on the screen was going to be a challenge. Trying to enter this world, to make it accessible to outsiders, would be an irresistible test. A rickshaw trundles elegantly past the window; a family is cooking on a busy street corner; bourgeois matrons sail grandly past a bony, scrofulous man who gestures at the sky with his fist while he communes with his personal gods. Black night, gold light, saris so blue you want to run them over your lips, saris so red they burn the backs of your eyes. Radios, the cry of a muezzin hanging in the air, raised voices from the shiny vault of a gold shop, and through it all slides the dull ring of the rickshaw puller's bell. This is the world I am about to try and enter, to recreate. I'm torn between terror and excitement.

Over the next weeks I begin a restless patrolling of the city, interviewing Catholic priests, Indian social workers, rickshaw *wallahs*, mafia leaders, police chiefs, doctors, pavement dwellers, scions of old families, poets, prostitutes, pimps, patients, and patriarchs. I love this time, this moment when imagination is tested against reality. With production designer Roy Walker and his team, we crisscross the city, stand on its corners, climb its stairs, clamber over its roofs. We squeeze through its Victorian alleys, between its construction sites, over

"One day we went and shot in the bustee, the actual Anand Nagar. People had put up a big banner and flowers at the entrance, saying "Welcome City of Joy," and they were celebrating and laughing. When I asked why they were so supportive, one man told me, 'This bustee been here for 40 years, and no one has ever been here, not even a politician. Now you come from thousands of miles away and walk our streets and smile at us and are friendly and interested—of course we're going to welcome you. And we're proud of our bustee.'

"In contrast to a slum, the implication of a bustee is that the residents are extraordinarily impoverished but will use anything—a stick, a piece of cloth, a rotting piece of corrugated iron, to make a house—things we would throw away. So although it's an image of poverty, it's also an image of great ingenuity. As you walk around, you marvel at the optimism of those who can use scraps of wood and iron to make a building. You're amazed by the resourcefulness of people who live in a brutalizing environment without letting themselves be brutalized."

Roland Joffé

its refuse heaps, and into its slums; perambulate through its parks and flower markets. We watch its bathers, its worshippers in their temples, its vendors, cobblers, butchers, *bidi* makers, tea sellers, water sellers, metalworkers, office *wallahs*, scavengers, child beggars and schoolchildren, refugees, tram drivers, ticket collectors, hoodlums, its drunks and drugged, its cyclists, cooks, sweepers, sign painters, priests, its porters and its poor, its sufferers and survivors . . . and above all its rickshaw pullers.

All these layers are analyzed, probed, savored on long dusty walks across the red New Mexico plain with the avidly curious writer, Mark Medoff, and in a flat in the Latin Quarter of Paris with co-writer Gérard Brach. To my surprise, I find myself making excuses for Calcutta—justifying, protecting, beginning to feel that an outsider can't understand.

I realize that I have fallen in love with this city on the marshland, in love with its unsung heroes and its villains. Yes, love—because nowhere else is the human condition writ so large; it is life. In its naked, shameless way, Calcutta mirrors what lies behind our struggles for order: this mess, this chaos, this divine concoction of indifference and cruelty and compassion; this humanness. Maybe this is what makes Satyajit Ray so protective of his city; he wants to shield its magnificent failings. No need for defensiveness, though. Calcutta speaks to people of all complexions because of its human frailties, not despite them.

Calcutta taught me to take nothing at face value. It taught me, in its complexity, its passion, anger, and pettiness, that our individual human failings are no more or less than failings of the species; as there are no perfect individuals, there are no perfect races. It taught me that the world is full of unexpected heroism. And it taught me that, though we are castaway from the moment we are born, engaged in a struggle to survive that ceases only with the end of life itself, true heroism lies in the quality of that struggle.

For your best and worst, which are also our best and worst, Calcutta, I salute you.

✣ City of Joy: A Producer's Journal ✣

by Jake Eberts

I am often asked how a film like *City of Joy* gets made. Where does the idea come from? How do the producer and director get together? How is the money raised? Most films are put together as a result of past relationships, experiences, shared tastes, and common goals. The following diary attempts to show how, why, and when these elements came together in *City of Joy*.

FEBRUARY 1968

My wife and I make our first visit to India, on our honeymoon. We do all the usual tourist things in and around New Delhi, but I know there is a lot we miss. Something about India touches my soul, and I long to return.

JANUARY 1977

I form my first film financing company, Goldcrest Films, and enjoy novice's luck. One of our first development investments turns out to be *Chariots of Fire*, directed by Hugh Hudson and produced by David Puttnam, who has a talent for spotting new directors. Two years later, David introduces me to another young director, Roland Joffé.

NOVEMBER 1980

Goldcrest commits to provide financing for Richard Attenborough's *Gandhi*, and I make the first of many trips to India to secure permission to film there. I meet many civil servants who will one day help me with *City of Joy*. Again I fall under the country's spell.

JANUARY 1982

I go back to India again, this time to set up *The Far Pavilions*, a combined feature film-TV miniseries to be shot in Rajasthan. I am more than ever drawn by India.

eggs.
March 1991

Imtiaz Dharker

MARCH 1982

Chariots of Fire wins the Academy Award for Best Picture, and I bask in reflected glory. I think I know what I'm doing and want to back more David Puttnam films. In January 1983 I get my chance with *The Killing Fields*, to be directed by Roland Joffé. I am very taken by Roland.

MARCH 1983

Gandhi wins eight Oscars including Best Picture; foreign tourists swarm to India. Hundreds of thousands of people share my fascination with this extraordinary land. The movie's success makes films about India more acceptable.

FEBRUARY 1984

Roland Joffé gets an Academy Award nomination for *The Killing Fields*. He becomes a "hot" young director.

SEPTEMBER 1985

I form a new company, Allied Filmmakers, having left Goldcrest late in 1983. I begin looking for new projects. My wife recommends that I read Dominique Lapierre's *The City of Joy*. (Seven years earlier I rejected her suggestion to go after rights to the novel *First Blood*, which other producers turned into the Rambo films, making centimillions for them. So this time I am obliged to listen to her.) I am overwhelmed by the book and immediately phone Lapierre to begin negotiating for the rights. Dominique wants to know who will direct the film. I tell him I have no idea, but Roland Joffé is in the back of my mind.

OCTOBER 1985

My old company, Goldcrest, gets into trouble, and I am asked to return part-time to help them out. One of their major projects is *The Mission*, being produced by David Puttnam and directed by Roland Joffé. I renew my acquaintance with Roland and a strong rapport starts to grow.

JANUARY 1986

Roland visits me in London during post-production of *The Mission*. We talk of future projects; though I am dying to be in business with Roland, at first I don't dare mention *The City of Joy* because I have not yet acquired the rights. As he leaves the meeting, he mentions as an aside that he is thinking of doing a film that most people would think him crazy to attempt. Intrigued by this mystery, I urge him to reveal what it is. Almost apologetically he tells me, *The City of Joy*. India's many gods are looking after me. I have found my director and fellow producer.

FEBRUARY 1986

Dominique Lapierre is ecstatic to learn that the renowned director of *The Killing Fields* is interested. Roland and I go to

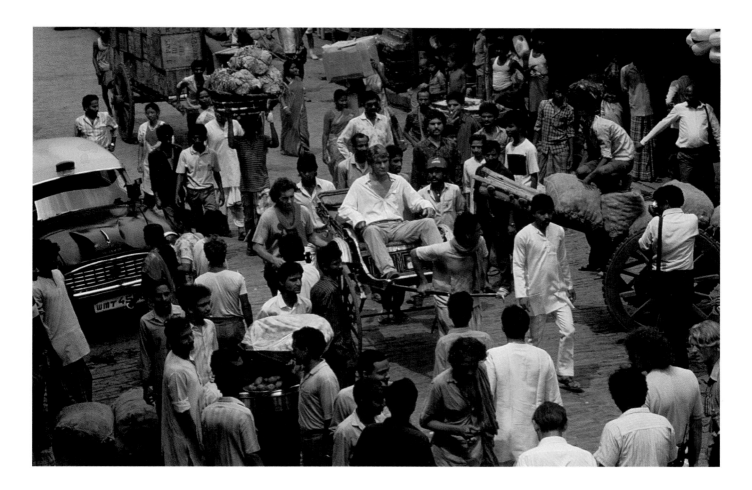

Paris to meet Dominique, and Roland's presence apparently clinches the deal for the rights. Detailed contract negotiations start.

Preparing to shoot the first scene of Hasari pulling Max in the rickshaw, amid Calcutta traffic.

MAY 1986

Negotiations with Dominique's lawyers drag on. To break the logjam, Roland and I meet with the author at his beautiful home near St. Tropez, coincidentally just as *The Mission* wins the Palme d'Or at Cannes. This finally convinces Dominique, and we sign the contract. Our plan is to hire a screenwriter immediately and begin shooting in February 1987, in the hope of releasing the film in time for Christmas 1987. Our budget target is $12 million.

SEPTEMBER 1987

Sixteen months have passed and we still have not found a writer. Understandably, Dominique is beginning to feel very frustrated. Roland's patience and persistence finally pay off when Mark Medoff agrees to do the screenplay. Not only is Mark mad keen on India, he has demonstrated with *Children of a Lesser God* the ability to write emotionally charged dialogue; we know he can provide the structure we need to create great drama out of simple situations. For the next two years, Mark writes and rewrites.

Patrick Swayze and Jake Eberts on the set.

APRIL 1989

I am beginning to run out of money, and no final screenplay is in sight. I turn to my friends Claude Berri and Paul Rassam in Paris, who agree to repay our development costs and give us a loan to cover future development costs, in return for French rights to the film. They also tentatively commit to lending us 100 percent of the production funding—provided we can get a U.S. distribution deal.

SEPTEMBER 1989

We are in constant touch with appropriate authorities in India to secure the permission needed before shooting can start. My contacts from *Gandhi* days are helpful, but it soon becomes clear that *The City of Joy* is far from universally admired in India. There are many expressions of opposition to our project from politicians, intellectuals, and journalists. Nonetheless we prevail in winning government approval to film in Calcutta. We begin constructing a massive set there and plan to start shooting in February 1990. Our budget has increased to $16.7 million, mainly because we have grossly underestimated labor and construction costs in India.

DECEMBER 1989

Mark has just about exhausted the various permutations and combinations regarding the main characters and principal sequences in the script, and delivers his seventh and final draft. While the character of Hasari is well defined in the book, Mark and Roland have had to develop Max Lowe virtually from scratch. They also must create a stronger and more linear story line for the two main characters. We submit the script to Warner Bros., which has always shown interest in the project.

JANUARY 1990

Warners is intrigued but will not give us a firm commitment, so shooting is postponed. They agree to continue funding development costs on condition that they own worldwide distribution rights. Claude and Paul are disappointed but graciously accept Warners' conditions. Roland and I have no alternative, and reluctantly bid adieu to Claude and Paul. The studio also insists on a revised screenplay, so Roland goes to Paris to work on a rewrite with Gérard Brach, as Mark is tied up with other commitments.

MAY 1990

India's federal government approves the revised, eleventh draft of the script, subject to review by certain intellectuals and local officials in Calcutta. Our budget has crept up to $18.3 million.

JUNE 1990

Roland delivers a twelfth draft to Warners; script discussions go on all summer. The studio still does not give us a final commitment. Mark Medoff comes back to help with the writing. Casting gets underway; we now plan to start shooting in November. We hire the crew and begin shipping equipment from London to Calcutta. The set is completely built and more than 60 people are on the payroll. If we do not make the picture, Allied will go bankrupt. Our budget has risen again, to $21.7 million, mainly due to the weakened dollar.

SEPTEMBER 1990

Disaster! Warners decides to pull out. We are given 30 days to refinance. Being unceremoniously dropped after five years hardly seems possible, but it is too late to stop the juggernaut. Shooting is postponed until February 1991 to give us a chance to regroup. Without a major studio behind us, we must fund production ourselves, which means extra contingency, interest, and insurance charges, raising our budget to $25 million—a far cry from the $12 million we projected.

This latest blow is almost enough to make us give up. But I have not counted on the lure of India and Calcutta's mesmerizing effect on everyone involved, particularly Roland. In desperation I turn again to my friends Claude and Paul; from one phone call and one meeting with their partner, Jerome Seydoux, comes an agreement to bail us out, contingent on our getting another U.S. distribution deal. Their word is backed up with an immediate loan of the funds needed to keep us going until shooting starts. In these days of computer-driven market research and conventional studio wisdom, it is hard to believe that such people still exist in our business. Their faith only increases our determination.

Co-producer Iain Smith.

OCTOBER 1990

Activity in Calcutta approaches fever pitch. Construction and rewrites continue, casting of Indian artists begins, budgets and schedules are done and redone. Many crew members who had been involved with *Gandhi* are as entranced by India as I am, and are anxious to relive the experience. Redoubtable line producer Iain Smith, who proved his mettle on *The Killing Fields* and *The Mission*, is once again pressed into service under impossible conditions. By now I have called on every major studio and only TriStar is remotely interested in U.S. rights. Again it looks as if we may have to shut down.

NOVEMBER 1990

As studio negotiations drag on, Patrick Swayze's agent contacts us. Although I am initially skeptical, Patrick's sincerity and commitment impress me. Roland is enthusiastic from the onset and, in the role of Max Lowe, Patrick proves to be absolutely terrific. Roland also signs Pauline Collins, a marvelous actress and a real trooper, for the part of Joan. The outstanding cast is rounded out by Om Puri and Shabana Azmi, two of India's most renowned actors.

Shooting the rickshaw pullers' strike scene with the mobile crane.

DECEMBER 1990

TriStar finally agrees to acquire North American distribution rights, but Roland and I have to mortgage our next project to cover any TriStar losses. We have no choice; by this time Allied has borrowed more than $14 million to keep pre-production going, and no other studio will make an offer.

FEBRUARY 1991

Production starts! The six years spent in getting the film to this point begin to seem like a picnic in comparison to what we encounter in Calcutta. The cast and crew are faced with riots, firebombs, government protests, lawsuits, and crowds marching in the streets. Campaigns by crusading journalists against the film are repulsed by Iain and Roland. Production must be stopped on four occasions.

MARCH 1991

I fly to Calcutta to seek a compromise with newspaper publishers, student agitators, lawyers, and Indian filmmakers, trying to use my *Gandhi* contacts to relieve the pressure. I am only partly successful.

May 1991

Somehow Roland and the cast and crew make it through, but at the expense of losing twelve days' shooting. Our stars are magnificent in their steadfast determination to complete the picture. We have to cut 25 scenes in order to get out of Calcutta in one piece. Of course we go over budget; I use profits from other films to cover the extra costs.

June 1991

Shooting is finished in Pinewood Studios, London, with additional pick-up shots done in Bombay. A Christmas release looks unlikely.

October 1991

Editing continues in London, with the music recorded in Rome. We are all entranced by the beauty of Ennio Morricone's score. We start preparing for previews; a December release is impossible, but we preview the film that month in New York and London. The response is excellent. As a result of these previews, we cut about 15 minutes, change the order of some scenes, and shoot a very short linking scene; some new music is added.

March 1992

Our picture is finally delivered, almost seven years after my wife told me about the book. During this time I have been involved with seven other films. It's hard to believe all these could have been made and released while we were struggling to get *City of Joy* on the screen. In the end, I think this film has given me the most satisfaction, maybe because I have had more to do with it than any of the others.

And that is how a film gets made.

❖ Screenwriter's Note ❖

by Mark Medoff

"Every storyteller is drawn to extremes. We look for what will enable us to connect with life. Storytellers give us mythical adventures that we can live through and feel without actually experiencing them."

Roland Joffé

As I write this, my involvement with *City of Joy* is almost at the beginning of its fifth year. It begins with the voice on our answering machine in Las Cruces, New Mexico, of Roland Joffé, whose work I know through his films *The Killing Fields* and *The Mission*. I'm aware through some show biz antenna that Joffé is preparing a movie about Los Alamos and the Manhattan Project called *Fat Man and Little Boy*.

Roland, on the answering machine, wants to know if I'll read a book by Dominique Lapierre about the poor of Calcutta, India. My first impulse is that, as an admirer of Lapierre (and his collaborations with Larry Collins), I'll be happy to read the book. My second impulse is that there's no way I want to spend several years living in my head in Calcutta while I try to make the book, whatever its substance or degree of difficulty, into a movie script.

A reading of Dominique's stunning book, filled with hundreds of vignettes, does nothing to change my mind. However, my wife, Stephanie, is unpretentiously into "signs" (though I am not). Based on Roland's voice on the answering machine and her own reading of the book, she urges me to say yes. I do.

For a long time, well over a year, I work alone while Roland rewrites, shoots, edits, and releases *Fat Man and Little Boy*. But as I look back on this experience, I see it as one in which a screenwriter and a film director learn how to work together, and finally to become true collaborators and friends.

Though there are hundreds of phone calls, overnight deliveries, fax communications between Los Angeles and Las Cruces, Calcutta and Las Cruces, London and Las Cruces, I remember most warmly the miles and miles we walk—through the cotton and chile fields of New Mexico, through Hyde Park and the Cotswolds in England, trying to create with this other human being a bond that will allow us together to make an intelligent entertainment, to tell well and relevantly and movingly the very human story of Max Lowe, Joan Bethel, and Hasari Pal and his family.

On my sixth movie, I experience for the first time with Roland a relationship akin to the one I'm accustomed to in the theater, where writer and director become inseparable parts of the work as a whole, and of each other's creative process. I also come to appreciate for the first time, without resentment or rancor, the weight on a film director's shoulders to be an amalgam of the creative, the managerial, the fiduciary, and the geological (for a film director indeed has to be a rock).

Even before the release of the finished film weeks or months from now, I know in my heart that we've made a success. Because we have done, without fear, through hours and days, months and finally years, the best we are capable of doing.

"Adversity is great, but mankind is greater than adversity."

Rabindranath Tagore

PROLOGUE

✦ EXILES ✦

✛ EXILES ✛

Dr. Max Lowe is a young neurosurgeon practicing in a hospital in Houston, Texas. His father, Alfred Lowe, is the medical director there, occupying an office in which he is surrounded by degrees and proclamations of his excellence. The two have a difficult relationship, yet it has always been Max's passionate wish to please his father in all things.

[Operating room]
Fierce white light. Heart and brain monitors. High tech. Figures gathered around: an anesthesiologist, scrub nurses. Dr. Max Lowe bends over a patient.

Something goes wrong. And we see now that the patient is a child, a young girl. The medical team works feverishly; Max performs heart massage in a last attempt to revive her. They fail. A nurse clips the tube that had connected the patient to a respirator.

[Hospital corridor]
Max is desperate, beyond outrage, beyond any normal range of rage itself. He strips off his surgical gown, slumping against the wall. Then he heads down the corridor, yanking off his mask, his eyes descending into some unseen hell. He is on his way to his father's office to tender his resignation. He intends never to set foot in a hospital again.

Patrick Swayze as Dr. Max Lowe.

The family of Hasari Pal has lived on the same farm in Bihar, a rural community in West Bengal, for generations. Their tiny plot is part of a larger farm formerly owned by Hasari's father. Once a prosperous peasant, the elder Pal and his wife have been forced to take shelter with his son's family after a series of misfortunes impoverished him.

Though poor, the Pals have a rich family life; besides the grandparents there are Hasari's wife, Kamla, and their children, Amrita (twelve, and the only daughter), ten-year-old Manooj, and six-year-old Shambu. Their half acre of good land grows barely enough rice to feed the family. This year, though, the monsoon was late. It spelled disaster for many such families living on the edge, as the young rice plants withered in the field.

At last Hasari determined to take his family to Calcutta, where he hoped to find work and send back money to his parents on the farm.

[A farm in Bihar]
The Pal family sits under the large tree at the top of the small well. Shambu, throwing stones into the well, keeps a lookout for the bus. Hasari's mother tries to comfort Kamla...

GRANDMOTHER
Don't be sad. Everything will be all right. You will have to be strong for your children. We will be all right here.

Hasari Pal, his wife, Kamla, and their daughter, Amrita.

A peasant uses a bullock team to draw water. Photo by Robert Holmes.

Exiled from the Land

"All around the hut the golden rice plantations stretched out as far as the eye could see," writes Dominique Lapierre of the Pals' family farm in Bihar, "sprinkled with the dark green of mango orchards, the light green of palm tree clusters and the soft green of bamboo groves. . . . Children with sticks drove great shining buffalo across the small dikes, stirring up ocher-colored dust as they went.

"'It was very pale, alluvial earth,' Hasari Pal would recall. 'But it was our earth, Mother Earth, Bhu-devi the goddess Earth.. . . . And if she suffers, we suffer with her.'"

Like millions of other Bengali peasants during the last half of the twentieth century, the Pals became victims of the cycle of poverty—"that unavoidable process of descending along the social ladder by which a farmer becomes a sharecropper, then a peasant without land, then an agricultural laborer, then, eventually forced into exile."

The Pals' troubles started with a greedy landowner cheated Hasari's father out of land he had inherited. The Pals' sons sharecropped another plot to make up for the food their remaining land could not produce, but were plagued with a rice parasite, forcing them into debt with the local *mahajan*, or jeweler-usurer, a key person in every village. Bad weather, the illness of Hasari's youngest brother, and the marriage of a sister added to their plight. They had to sell nearly all of their livestock and turn to the moneylender again, borrowing against the next harvest.

The final blow came when the monsoon would not. First more money was spent for a priest to celebrate a *puja* to bring the rain, then to hire an irrigation pump. All to no avail: "The rice drooped, then wilted and finally died—the very rice that they had nursed, caressed and loved."

The remaining cow nearly perished, and cattle merchants swooped in to buy the village's starving animals for next to nothing. Finally the well the villagers used for drinking water dried up, and the migration to the city that had started as a trickle became a flood—and the Pals were part of it.

Dominique Lapierre,
The City of Joy

The Pals' sons, Shambu and Manooj.

Cousin Bansi has promised to look after us. So don't worry. Don't worry.

Hasari's father reassures her.

GRANDFATHER
Come on. Don't worry. Eat something. We'll be all right, Baba. Come on, eat something.

The old man turns to Hasari.

GRANDFATHER
Have you kept the address with you for safety?

HASARI
Yes, Baba.

GRANDFATHER
What if you don't get work immediately?

HASARI
I will, Baba. So many people go to the city every day. Stop worrying.

GRANDFATHER
I am worrying because I want to see Amrita married before I die.

Shambu runs acros the road.

SHAMBU
Baba! Baba! The bus.

HASARI
The bus is coming.

The bus arrives. The family gather their possessions together and go towards the bus. Hasari passes up their possessions to a man on top of the bus.

HASARI
Be careful, please.

"Ovid was wrong when he wrote 'There is nothing permanent in the world except change.' In rural India, in the villages of Bengal, change is an alien concept: that rickety bullock cart, the same iron plow, the changeless, bony skeletons wrapped tight in dark shiny skin, endure immutably. Mud huts and dung cakes still provide fuel as they did centuries ago. Everywhere one turns, there is fathomless pain, in unblinking eyes, the deep expressionless stares of those who have plumbed the depths and transcended despair."

Sasthi Brata,
India: Labyrinths in Lotus Land

Kamla, holding some of the Pals' few possessions, worries about what their new life in Calcutta will bring as the bus bears them away.

(turns to Shambu)
You go sit in the bus.

Kamla and the children get onto the bus. Hasari's mother gives the children last instructions.

GRANDMOTHER
Behave like a good girl. Try to help your mother.
(to Shambu)
You two, don't fight each other. And Manooj, stay away from the cinema.

Hasari's father crosses to him. Hasari is finishing off instructions to the man up top.

HASARI
Not there. Put it here and tie that bundle to the rod.
(as his father joins him)
Don't worry about Amrita. I will be saving money for her dowry. You will come for her wedding.

GRANDFATHER
Yes.

HASARI
And I will send you money and I will write to you soon.

GRANDFATHER
A man's journey to the end of his obligation is a very long road.

PART I

✦ Planting the Seeds ✦

✤ Planting the Seeds ✤

[Howrah Station, Calcutta]

Early morning. A huge bridge dominates the skyline as the train from Bihar pulls in. A uniformed band plays on the station platform.

The train trundles to a stop, its whistle clearing the way. People hang on its sides, sit on the roof. And now they flood the platform, flowing into the station, clearing a view for us of the Pals, clinging to their baggage in the middle of this human anthill. Hands reach out with sweets or tea to sell, begging money.

The family (and we) are overwhelmed by the desperate energy of the humanity around them. As they press on, Kamla senses someone: a beggar, face half-hidden and eaten away by leprosy. This terrifying image presses the boys tightly to their mother. Hasari moves to wrap the family inside the embrace of his arms. It doesn't seem possible that he can protect all of them against the predatory eyes watching them.

He moves them quickly to a wall and tells them to wait as he crosses to a vendor's stall and shows his precious piece of paper.

HASARI

Please, can you tell me this address? This is my friend Niranjah. We are to stay with him.

VENDOR 1

I don't think there is any such address as this in Calcutta.

The vendor gives the address a look, gives it back to Hasari. The other vendor takes it.

HASARI

But that's not possible.

Like other displaced families, the Pals take refuge temporarily in the railroad station.

VENDOR 1

Of course it is possible! Who lives here, you or me? Who knows if a place exists or does not?

VENDOR 2

You go Bombay, perhaps. Try Delhi. Try the moon.

VENDOR 1

(laughing)

Yes, try the moon.

[A spartan room at an ashram]

INDIAN WOMAN

So things went wrong for you, Max. But do you think life will be any better if you turn your back on it? Your hostility is why we asked you to leave—that was quite a commotion you caused yesterday. How long have you been here, Max?

MAX

Three days.

INDIAN WOMAN

Why did you come here?

Contrasting with the desperate poor crowding Howrah Station, notables arriving by train are often greeted by colorfully uniformed bands.

"Howrah station is an experience. At the entrance there is a notice in English and Hindi which reads 'We hope you have a happy journey.' Inside the station portals lie the bodies of the destitute who have nowhere to live or die, children, babies; many are refugees from Bangladesh— this is now their only home."

Frances Meigh, *Destitutes of Calcutta*

Max receives and rejects good counsel at the ashram.

MAX
(almost inaudibly)
Burnt out. Had a friend who came. Was a big mistake.

INDIAN WOMAN
No, Max. We end up where we are meant to be.

MAX
Give me a break, lady.

INDIAN WOMAN
Do you always require instant answers?
(She picks up a tea pot and cup and hands cup to Max.)
Here is your tea.

MAX
I don't want it.

INDIAN WOMAN
Come. Sit down.

She leads him to the bed, sits beside him, and pours the tea till it runs over the top.

MAX
What are you doing?

INDIAN WOMAN
How can you be filled up if you are not empty?

Patrick Swayze as Dr. Max Lowe

Starring as Max, the doctor who finds a new commitment to life through his love for Hasari Pal and the people of the City of Joy, is Patrick Swayze. It is an emotionally demanding part that represents a new stage in the actor's fast-moving career.

Like Max Lowe, Swayze grew up in Houston, Texas, where his mother was a dance teacher and choreographer. Swayze excelled early as a dancer and athlete, and studied with the Harkness and Joffrey ballet companies before beginning his acting career.

His early film roles were in the action-adventure mold, and an appearance in the Civil War miniseries *North and South* brought him national recognition. His breakthrough role in *Dirty Dancing* in 1987 earned him a Golden Globe nomination for best actor, and the success of this film combined with his starring role in the 1990 hit *Ghost* made him one of America's top stars. Swayze's other films include *Point Break, Road House,* and *Red Dawn.*

Of the search for an actor to play Max, director Roland Joffé says , "I wanted someone who could discover himself and needed an actor who would be discovered by the audience. *Dirty Dancing* was a beautifully acted film—watch Patrick's performance and how he affects the people around him. Some actors create an energy that everyone lives off; Patrick is that sort of actor. He's tough and disciplined, and he was ready to take on a risky film."

For Swayze, Max is the part he has been working toward all his life. "I think one reason Roland cast me is that, aside from my needs and desires as an actor, as a person I needed this experience," he says. "I needed a shot in the arm to focus the self-exploration I'd been going through.

"I went through a real metamorphosis in Calcutta. My first reaction was sympathy, for the terrible conditions these people live under, but I soon realized that was the last thing they wanted. What stayed with me is amazement at the resiliency of human spirit: how they can live through it all and love life still. It was astounding that people with nothing would share their last bowl of rice with you or offer a smile that could light up the universe.

"Their religious beliefs may have a lot to do with it; they almost seem to feel it's a privilege to go through what they do. And the longer I was there, the more kinship I felt with the people. You realize that emotionally everyone is in the same life condition and has the same problems to work though on earth."

Swayze found it easy to identify with Max Lowe's reaction to life in the City of Joy. "The very thing that confused me was the same thing that needed to confuse Max—he doesn't understand how they can allow themselves to suffer and be exploited because he comes from a fight-back point of view. So Max learns a big lesson and Patrick learned a big lesson through this process. At first I passionately believed that these people had to fight back, but as time went on, I came to see that maybe the way they fight—in terms of personal revolution and personal enlightenment—may be the best way. It did a lot toward making me not just talk a good line about becoming more of a pacifist, but really believing it can work.

"I sometimes feel as if I went there as Patrick and came back as Max. I'm not even quite sure who I'm speaking as now!"

Like many who go to Calcutta, Swayze finds that he is haunted by it. "To be in Calcutta for any length of time you have to make choices. It's very easy to shut yourself off, and the key to Max—which I found through Roland's guidance—is that he loses the ability to shut it out. At that point, you either go crazy or you come to a new revelation about yourself and the world.

"The longer I'm away from Calcutta, the more I miss it," Swayze says simply. "I dream about the place. I'm still working through what it did to me and probably will be for a long time."

Mr. Gangooly approaches the Pals in the Bara Bazaar.

"For Hasari Pal and the millions of exiles who crowded into its slums . . . Calcutta represented neither culture nor history. For them it meant only the faint hope of finding some crumbs to survive until the next day. In a metropolis of such magnitude there were always a few crumbs to be gathered, whereas in a village flooded with water or parched by drought, even that possibility didn't exist anymore. . . ."

Dominique Lapierre,
The City of Joy

Leaving Howrah Station, the Pals thread their way cautiously through Calcutta's insane traffic. After wandering in bewilderment a short while, they are directed to a place by the Hooghly River where many of Calcutta's homeless camp out. That night, as they watch a corpse being pulled from the river, Hasari tries to reassure the children that he will find work very soon.

Over the next several days, he roams through the street bazaars, alternately trying to find someone who recognizes their friend's address and asking for work. The family trails behind, hauling their possessions. Discouraged, they stop for refreshment at a tea vendor's stall.

The Pals are scared, dispirited, weary. They've been walking a long time. As Hasari gets out his little screw of money to pay for tea, he is watched by a man named Gangooly, who crosses over to them.

GANGOOLY
Hello, boys! Hey, are you from Bihar?

HASARI
Yes.

GANGOOLY
I am also from Bihar! Is that your family? You look worried. It is not necessary. Thank the lord. And Mr. Gangooly.

Gangooly unleashes a smile as full as the sky above.

❖

[Green Acres Hotel]

Across the street, a group of children are playing in a water pump. A little girl comes toward Max with a luminous smile, her hand out. Something ignites inside Max somewhere, and he puts a gentle hand to the girl's cheek. Leaves it there, his eyes fixed on her, for what seems a long moment.

MAX
Okay. Coin. Watch.

Max reaches behind the girl's ear, extracts a rupee.

MAX
There it is, for you.

Unwittingly, he's made a mistake. The other children start clamoring in Hindi and, within seconds, he's surrounded by a pushing, begging swarm of children, many hands reaching for him, grabbing at his hands. He backs away, heads across the street.

A porter hurries out of the hotel to meet him, screaming in Hindi at the children to leave the *sahib* alone. Max follows the porter in through the gates, pushing between two cows blocking the entrance.

Max is guided through the walled and well-planted courtyard into the lobby of this inexpensive hotel.

MAX
What's your name?

PORTER
Ishmail.

> "The average European was not conditioned to live with beggary of this nature in the middle of the twentieth century. . . . At first his conscience troubles him so much that he dispenses charity to all who approach him. But the, one day, a woman to whom he has given all his loose change counts it carefully and pursues him angrily for more; he finds himself looking carefully over his shoulder, before tossing coin in yet another bowl, to see how many of the beggar's fellows are within pouncing distance; and before long he is giving very selectively indeed. As long as he remains in Calcutta he is emotionally split in two by the children who come at him and will not let him go, as though he were a second Pied Piper."
>
> Geoffrey Moorhouse,
> *Calcutta*

Max with begging children outside the Green Acres. Overleaf: *The Pals camp by the Hooghly River as a body is found in the water.*

MAX
Ishmail with a smile. . . . Hello, hello.

The manageress radiates a smile.

MANAGERESS
Welcome, sir. How many nights?

MAX
Uno noche. One night.

MANAGERESS
May I see your passport, please?

MAX
You certainly may.

Max pats his pockets, searches his bag. No passport.

MAX
Oh, shit. . . . I must have left it at the ashram.

MANAGERESS
I'm sure it can be sorted out.

Gangooly leads the Pals through the crowded streets to a nearby building in a working-class section of the city, and unlocks the door of a small room. He opens the shutters; the room floods with light. He turns to Hasari.

GANGOOLY
The place is yours for a month. My cousin Moti is away. See the room. I believe you will like it. Normally the rent takes four hundred rupees for a month. Come, sit. For a brother, three hundred. No, don't thank me!

Hasari pulls out his little screw of money. Kamla, on the step outside, watches, still a little apprehensive.

HASARI
No, see. I have only two hundred.

GANGOOLY
Give me the two hundred, pay the rest next week. You'll find work, I trust you. Aren't I from Bihar, too? Yes!

And the money is in his pocket. He joins his hands together.

GANGOOLY
You are pleased? Then Mr. Gangooly is pleased! It's how I am.

And he's gone. Kamla joins Hasari, the relief slowly flooding over her face. Outside, much laughter as Amrita and Manooj pour a bucket of water over the unsuspecting Shambu.

"Hundreds of poor luckless families strayed like this father and his children through the same labyrinth, hoping for the same miracle: the discovery of a compatriot from their village, their district, their province, a relative, an acquaintance, the friend of a friend, a member of their caste . . . in short, someone who might be prepared to take them under his protective wing and find them two or three hours, perhaps a whole day, or even—miracle of miracles—several days of work. This ceaseless quest was not quite as unrealistic as it might appear. Every individual in India is always linked to the rest of the social body by a network of incredibly diversified ties, with the result that no one in this gigantic country of seven hundred fifty million inhabitants could ever be completely abandoned— except, perhaps, for Hasari Pal, whom this 'inhuman city' seemed obstinately to reject."

Dominique Lapierre,
The City of Joy

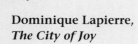

Max outside the Green Acres Hotel.

[Max's room at the Green Acres]
The light is turned on in the shuttered and utterly utilitarian room, sending an army of cockroaches scurrying. Max clearly doesn't care for cockroaches. The porter turns on the ceiling fan.

PORTER
It pleases you?

MAX
No fruit basket? No mini bar?

Max hands the Porter several rupees.

PORTER
Bar? Of course, many. But make care, Sahib. Please, for me. If you like drink, come to me below. If it is lady you like to know, you tell me. Yes? Very sweet girl, good nature, very sweet.

Max puts a finger on the Porter's head, turns him, and eases him, smiling nonstop, out the door.

MAX
I don't need a lady. What I need is a bath.

PORTER
Or boy, very good, very . . .

"Every dawn . . . began with a general process of purification. There, in alleyways awash with slime, beside the disease-ridden stream of a sewer, the occupants of the City of Joy banished the miasma of the night with all the ritual of a meticulous toilet. Without revealing so much as a patch of their nudity, the women managed to wash themselves all over, from their long hair to the soles of their feet, not forgetting their saris. After that, they would take the greatest care to oil, comb, and braid their hair, before decorating it with a fresh flower picked from God knows where. At every water point, men were showering themselves with tins. Young boys cleaned their teeth with acacia twigs coated with ashes, old men polished their tongues with strands of jute, mothers deloused their children before soaping their little naked bodies. . . Neither the biting winter cold nor the pangs of an empty stomach would accelerate the completion of this ancestral ritual of purification, which young and old piously adhered to each morning."

Dominique Lapierre,
The City of Joy

*A young boy washes in the street.
Photo by Dominique Lapierre.*

MAX
No, bath. Bath. Here you go.
(hands him a tip)
Thank you, Ishmail.

Max opens his bag. On top are some pamphlets the Indian woman gave him, rubber-banded together. He sits on the bed and flips through them: guides to inner peace.

MAX
(with distaste)
Meditate on this.

He wings the pamphlets, then the letter, at the trashcan.

[The Pals' new lodging]
There's laughter off camera from Kamla and Amrita. Joyful shouts from the boys.

Hasari is alone in the main room, on his knees, in front of the pile of their baggage and bundles. He turns his attention to a just-opened old suitcase. He takes out a small tea box. Opens it delicately. It's full of something brown. He pushes his fingers in and feels this bit of earth with a tenderness that's almost religious, puts a pinch to his nose, and breathes it in. The laughter and shouting from the bathing area are growing.

Outside the house, Shambu paddles near the tap. Kamla bends over the drain, and Amrita rinses her heavy, dark hair with a pot. Manooj is nearby, rubbing

himself with an old towel. Hasari enters unnoticed and looks at the group with tenderness, and with gratitude for their good fortune.

A man yanks the curtain aside. The family freezes. Kamla's hair drips unnoticed on her sari.

MAN
What are you doing here? Who are you?

HASARI
My name is Pal, Hasari. Mr. Gangooly rented this space to . . .

MAN
Mr. Who?

HASARI
Gangooly. You must be his cousin, Mr. Moti.

Roland Joffé's storyboard art for the sequence described on these pages. On most films a professional artist sketches out the director's ideas for each scene, but Joffé drew his own for City of Joy.

Opposite page: Hasari dreams of home as he fingers the earth he has brought from Bihar.

MAN

I don't know any Gangooly, and my name is Binal, and this is my home. Get out!

The furious Binal and his wife, followed by the Pals, go into the main part of the room. A small crowd has been attracted by the noise.

HASARI

But this is true. We gave him all our money. He said the rent . . .

BINAL

A man goes out because he has to work, and some beggar tries to move in while his back is turned!

Binal has begun to throw things out onto the street, though this cleansing of his home doesn't stop him from picking up a stick.

BINAL

You're lucky I don't kill you!

Hasari looks at Manooj, who drops his eyes. They collect their possessions and hurry out the door, Binal pursuing them down the street.

The Pals back on the street after Binal throws them out of his house.

[Max's room]

It is night. Max sits on the side of the bath, the shower head dripping. Max is in deep thought. There's a knock on the door.

MAX
Just a minute.

He crosses the room and opens the door. The porter pushes Poomina gently into the room. She is beautiful and exotic-looking behind her excessive make-up. The porter smiles at Max, nodding.

PORTER
She is sweet girl.
(to Poomina)
Mr. Max is American. Very disciplined!

He slides out the door and closes it, over Max's protests. The girl stares at Max.

MAX
What's your name?

POOMINA
Poomina.

MAX
How old are you, Poomina?

POOMINA
Twenty, Sahib.

MAX
I buy that.

He tries to open the door. She pushes against it, then moves quickly to pour him a beer. She holds out the beer; reluctantly he takes it. Having gained this advantage, she takes him by the arm.

A courtesan of Kalighat (Calcutta), painted c. 1890. From Kalighat Paintings.

"Next they entered one of Calcutta's red-light districts. Women with provocatively colored skirts, low-cut bodices, and outrageously made-up faces were talking and laughing. Hasari was struck dumb with astonishment. He had never seen such creatures in his life, for where he came from the women wore only saris. 'Several of them called out to me. There was one I found very attractive. She must have been very rich because her arms were covered in bracelets right up to her elbows.'

". . . [Ram] took advantage of the incident to give his companion a warning: 'If ever you're pulling a rickshaw and you happen to get a girl like that for a fare, don't forget to make her pay in advance. Otherwise, mind you, she'll slip through your fingers just like an eel.'"

Dominique Lapierre,
The City of Joy

MAX
No.

POOMINA
Is problems, Sahib?

MAX
Yeah. Is problems.

Poomina shrugs her shoulders and crosses to the bed, looks about for another idea. She sees Max's cigars, crosses over to them and holds a cigar out to Max, again taunting him. Giving up, he moves toward the bed.

[A dark street]
The Pal family huddles at the foot of a wall on a filthy street with several other indigent families, across from a billboard ironically advertising a luxurious couch. After their humiliating flight, they found refuge here.

Hasari crosses to Kamla and sits next to her. She covers him with part of a meager blanket.

KAMLA
I remember the first day I saw you, on the day of our marriage. You were wearing a bright yellow turban. You asked me my name and said, "You are a very beautiful girl, and I am wondering whether you will find me appealing."

Hasari sighs and glances upward.

HASARI
Maybe the god is taking a test.

KAMLA
I feel I'm such a burden. In the village I could be of use.
(a beat)
Maybe the children and I should go out to the cars.

HASARI

You mean beg? We didn't come here to beg.

She puts her head on his shoulder.

Poomina takes Max to a back-alley bar, where a band plays a Western song in quavering Indian tones. Max performs sleight-of-hand tricks for Poomina as they drink. She engages him in a drinking contest, which he joins in all too willingly.

They are closely observed by a dangerous young gangster named Ashoka—the son of a local zamindar, or godfather—who is there with the Goonda (an enforcer) and other henchmen. In fact, Poomina works for Ashoka and has reluctantly lured Max to the bar on his orders.

Max sings "Take It to the Limit" with enormous inebriated sincerity as Poomina helps him out of the bar. There's a big black motorcycle parked outside. Max glances at it as they start down the alley. As he looks back to the road ahead, he finds the Goonda in front of him. Max isn't so drunk that he doesn't sense what this is about. He looks behind him. Indeed, the other two goons are there. Ashoka straddles the big cycle.

Max is mugged in the alley by Ashoka's men.

"A slum was not exactly a shanty-town. It was more like a sort of poverty-stricken industrial suburb inhabited exclusively by refugees from rural areas. Everything in these slums combined to drive their inhabitants to abjection and despair: shortage of work and chronic unemployment, appallingly low wages, the inevitable child labor, the impossibility of saving, debts that could never be redeemed, the mortgaging of personal possessions and their ultimate loss sooner or later. There was also the total nonexistence of any reserve food stocks and the necessity to buy in minute quantities . . . and the total absence of privacy with ten or twelve people sharing a single room. Yet the miracle of these concentration camps was that the accumulation of disastrous elements was counterbalanced by other factors that allowed their inhabitants not merely to remain fully human but even to transcend their condition and become models of humanity.

"In these slums people actually put love and mutual support into practice. They knew how to be tolerant of all creeds and castes, how to give respect to a stranger, how to show charity toward beggars, cripples, lepers, and even the insane. Here the weak were helped, not trampled upon. Orphans were instantly adopted by their neighbors and old people

(continued, page 49)

MAX
Well, well. Seek punishment and ye shall find.

Knowing what's coming, Max nevertheless unleashes a bestial howl and tries to trample the Goonda off-tackle. From behind, he's hit with a length of stick. He goes down, looks up through blasted eyes at Ashoka as two sticks now land against his shoulder and his head.

[The Pals' patch of street]
The family sleeps. Hasari awakens to the sound of a fight. The others awaken. Hasari gets up.

ANOTHER MAN
Don't go. What are you doing?

HASARI
It sounds like someone needs help.

Hasari bolts from the corner. As he turns into the alley, he sees three men beating someone, a fourth standing off to the side watching.

HASARI
What are you doing?
(calling back)
A man's being beaten here!

As Hasari runs down the alley, the motorcycle fires up and screams off, and the three goons take flight. One rips a medallion and chain from around Max's neck as he goes.

Hasari tries to help Max to his feet. As Hasari touches him, Max turns and belts Hasari in the nose, nailing Hasari to the wall. Max collapses at Hasari's feet. Hasari grabs his nose with one hand and kneels beside the fallen Max, as Poomina steps into the light.

POOMINA
I know where we can take him.

Pauline Collins as Joan Bethel.

[The dispensary, City of Joy]

A crucifix is seen from Max's POV. The crucifix sways. Now Max's eyes focus on the cherubic face of Joan Bethel, peering at the camera.

Max is on a cot in a tiny room, a butterfly bandage over one eye. Joan, fifty and attractive in a simple, no-nonsense Irish way, hovers over him. Behind her is Hasari Pal.

JOAN
Hey Junior, welcome to India.

Max raises a hand to his aching head. He manages to sit up.

MAX
Where am I?

JOAN
You're in the City of Joy.

MAX
Is that geographic or spiritual?

JOAN
I'd say that depends on your point of view. This is the gentleman who brought you in.

Max feels for his watch and chain.

JOAN
Whoever it was, they will have cleaned you out, I'm afraid.

Joan opens the medicine cupboard, begins putting back medicines. Max looks up and sees Hasari in the open doorway.

MAX
Did I do that to your nose?
(Hasari nods)
I'm very sorry.

Hasari shrugs, smiles. A little girl appears with Max's washed shirt.

GIRL
Auntie Joan.

Joan crosses the little room to her and holds out the shirt to Max, helping him to slip it on.

JOAN
What brings you to India?

MAX
Came to find enlightenment.

JOAN
And did you find it?

were cared for and revered by their children.

"Unlike the occupants of shantytowns in other parts of the world, in these slums the former peasants who took refuge there were not marginals. They had reconstructed the life of their villages in their urban exile. An adapted and disfigured life perhaps—but nonetheless so real that their poverty itself had become a form of culture. The poor of Calcutta were not uprooted. They shared in a communal world and respected its ancestral traditions and beliefs. Ultimately—and this was of primary importance—they knew that if they were poor it was not their fault, but the fault of the cyclical or permanent maledictions that beset the places where they came from.

"One of the principal and oldest of Calcutta's slums was situated in the suburbs, a fifteen minutes' walk from the railway station where the Pal family first alighted. It was wedged between a railway embankment, the Calcutta-Delhi highway, and two factories. Either out of ignorance or defiance, the jute factory owner who, at the beginning of the century, had lodged his workers on this land which he had reclaimed from a fever-infested marsh, had christened the place Anand Nagar, 'City of Joy.'"

Dominique Lapierre,
The City of Joy

MAX
Keep opening the doors and windows of my soul, but haven't seen a damned thing yet.

Max is irritated by Joan's ministerings, shrugs her off, and lurches for the door, buttoning his shirt, his entire body revolting. Too late Joan thinks to say:

JOAN
Mind your—

Max cracks his already aching head on the door frame.

MAX
Thanks. Got it.

He ducks outside for some air. In the dawn light, he finds himself in a small square in a slum, an open sewer running before him. Max is stunned. Squinting. Hallucinating, surely.

MAX
Jesus H. Christ!

Trying to orient himself, Max turns as Joan comes out of clinic, followed by Hasari.

MAX
(to Joan)
You a doctor?

JOAN
Nah . . . corporate executive.

Max follows Joan as she walks towards the square.

JOAN
We have a young intern who comes in three days a week at seven thirty.

MAX
This is obviously one of those three days.

JOAN
It is.

Joan stops to look and talk to a mother and baby in a group of perhaps two dozen people, largely women and children, waiting for the doctor.

JOAN
Namesgar. I'll see him later.

Joan moves on, Max following.

MAX
This is the dispensary?

JOAN
Humble though it is.

Margareta and a young pupil greet Joan. Ram, by his house, is cleaning his rickshaw.

JOAN
What is it that you do in America?

Max is slow to answer. Hasari keeps a discreet distance.

JOAN
God. You're very titillating. Are you a criminal of some sort?

MAX
Depends how you define the word: I was a doctor.

JOAN
Go 'way. How long are you . . .

MAX
And don't try to recruit me, lady. You've got your nonpracticing Catholics, I'm a nonpracticing doctor. So if you could just point me toward the hotel.

Surya, from the tea shop, passes and takes a good look at them.

JOAN
Why don't you practice?

MAX
Because I just don't like sick people.
(turning to leave)
Thank you. I owe you one.

Max and Joan at the City of Joy Self-Help Dispensary and School, which Joan runs on less than a shoestring.

Ganesh enthroned; his vehicle, the rat, beneath, c. 1885. From Kalighat Paintings.

"Hasari Pal stood and gazed at the rickshaw before him, as if it were Ganesh in person—Ganesh the elephant-headed god, benefactor of the poor who brought good fortune and removed obstacles."

Dominique Lapierre,
The City of Joy

JOAN
Yeah.

Max turns his bleary eyes on Hasari.

MAX
Listen . . .

He fumbles in his pockets for his money.

HASARI
No, no please.

Max finds his pockets empty.

JOAN
When they clean you out here, they do a good job.
(She crosses over to Ram.)
Ram, here's your first rider.
(to Max)
Here. Ah, go on. It's all right.
She holds out several rupee notes. Ram runs off with his rickshaw.

JOAN
You'll owe me two.

Max and Hasari turn and follow Ram and his rickshaw up the lane.

MAX
You live back here?

HASARI
No. I am new to the city.

MAX
Where you from?

HASARI
I am from Bihar.

Max and Hasari come out into the street from the alley by the shrine, followed by Ram pulling the rickshaw.

MAX
Well, you sure picked one hell of a city.

Hasari turns to Ram, an anxious look on his face.

HASARI
Do you think it be possible for me to pull one of these?

RAM
What?! You think any idiot can pull one of these rickshaws?

Ram stops in the middle of the busy street.

HASARI
I learn fast. Let me try.

MAX

Give him a try. He's as fast as you, and you should take care of that ankle.

HASARI

Please. You let me try.

MAX

Let him try. I'll let you have the full fare.

Max jumps up into the rickshaw.

RAM

All right. But it's your responsibility.

Hasari slides between the shafts. Tries to pull, but the center of gravity isn't easy to find. The rickshaw tips up. Hasari's feet leave the ground, Max dips backward dangerously, and Ram yanks him back to earth. People close by laugh. Hasari looks guiltily at Max.

MAX

Okay . . . make us look good, farmer!

Hasari nods at Max; they're a team. He strains forward. The rickshaw moves. People watch. Ram limps alongside, shouting instructions and oaths. The traffic

The veteran puller Ram Chander guides Hasari on his maiden trip through Calcutta traffic.

Debotosh Ghosh, who plays the role of Ram Chander, a rickshaw puller and Hasari's mentor, says, "There is no such thing as a big or small role. A good actor can prove his worth even in a minor role."

is going nuts. They make their way through the maelstrom, an avalanche of oaths following them, Max cheering Hasari on.

[Green Acres Hotel]
Hasari runs in with the rickshaw, Max giving running commentary. They stop with a flourish the courtyard. Hasari is panting, utterly exhausted but proud. Ram runs up, looks at him with respect.

MAX
Hooah! Good job, Hasari.
(turns to Ram)
Good man. Okay.

His head aching, Max gets out. Turns to Hasari.

MAX
Thanks. Good luck.

Hasari nods and smiles at Max. With the porter, Max heads inside.

PORTER
Mr. Max, did you have a good night?

MAX
Memorable. Has my passport arrived yet?

The porter shakes his head. Max approaches the landlady, wearing his best smile.

MAX
I think I may be about to have a little problem with the bill. . . .

The porter shouts at Hasari and Ram, as Ram turns the rickshaw.

HASARI
Excuse me.

Ram moves to give him his share of the money.

HASARI
No. No. I need some work.

RAM
So . . .

HASARI
I need some work. I have a family.

Ram looks hard at him.

RAM
Come.

He pockets the money and runs off, Hasari following.

[Throne room, the Godfather's house]

Ashoka, sitting with his thugs by a billiards table packed with an assortment of dusty papers, sees Hasari and Ram waiting.

Poomina, holding a kitten, comes toward the verandah, sees Hasari and stops short, laying a finger on her lips for silence. She disappears.

Ashoka moves to the verandah where they wait, pocketing the money laid out on a small table. Ashoka sits behind his leger. The Godfather, Mr. Ghatak, is seen in background being attended to by his servant.

ASHOKA
So he wants to be a human horse?

RAM
Yes, Babu.

ASHOKA
Does he not have a mouth?
(to Hasari)
Can you neigh? Neigh like a horse?

Ashoka pulls back his lips, shows his teeth, and imitates a neigh: "Ne-igh! Ne-igh!"

ASHOKA
Go on.

Ghatak lectures Hasari about loyalty as his servant stands ready with the pan *box.*

Ram and Hasari visit the Godfather to ask if Hasari can join his stable of rickshaw pullers.

> "*Pan*, those subtle quids made out of a little finely chopped betel nut, a pinch of tobacco, a suggestion of lime, chutney, and cardamom, all rolled up in a betel leaf skillfully folded and sealed with a clove. *Pan* gave energy. Above all, it curbed the appetite."
>
> Dominique Lapierre,
> *The City of Joy*

Behind Ashoka, his father walks to his chair. Barely glancing at his son, he waves him out of the chair.

ASHOKA
He wants a rickshaw.

Ghatak chews on a piece of pan and casts a benevolent eye on Hasari. His attentive servant holds out his pan box, which he helps himself to.

GHATAK
Lift your dhoti. Pull up your vest. Take a deep breath.

Hasari does. The Zamindar looks at his legs and thighs.

GHATAK
Acha, age has not fed off you yet! They say that nirvana is the attainment of a state of supreme detachment. For me, nirvana is counting each evening, one by one, the rupees brought by my two thousand and forty-six rickshaws.

Hasari doesn't know whether to respond. A glance at Ram tells him not to.

GHATAK
You are with family?

HASARI
Yes, Babu. A wife and three children.

GHATAK
And they must eat, heh? The world is full of open mouths.

He chews on this a moment, then gestures to Ashoka, who gets out a small, tinkling bell. The Godfather holds it out toward Hasari and then throws it to him. Hasari understands that, incredibly, he has a job. He can barely utter his gratitude.

GHATAK
Stay loyal.

The Human Horses and Their Chariots of Fire

Calcutta is the last place where the hand-drawn rickshaw survives. The red and black, two-wheeled carriages with their thin, undernourished drivers ringing tiny bells to attract customers are a familiar sight on the city's decaying streets. Many thousands of Calcutta's pavement and slum dwellers scratch out a living by pulling other people around the streets: "a job no human being should be asked to do," says Roland Joffé. But that is the job of Hasari Pal in *City of Joy*.

Hasari, who, like many of his real-life counterparts, comes to Calcutta to escape drought in his native Bihar, is delighted when the local godfather allows him into his fleet of rickshaw pullers. It means money honorably earned to feed his wife and children. He also knows that, in a city where hundreds of thousands are condemned to living on the streets, a hundred other poor peasants are waiting to take his place should he fail.

To prepare for his role as Hasari, Om Puri spent three weeks training under the benevolent eyes of two rickshaw pullers. From a half hour on his first day, he built up to a three-hour barefoot run through the early morning traffic. "I had to show that I felt comfortable with the rickshaw," Puri says. "One should not indulge in professional cheating, like using someone else's feet.

"Every morning at six a.m. I took the rickshaw out with two mock passengers. At first I wore my jogging suit but realized I was drawing too much attention, so I wore a *lungi* (a long, wraparound garment) and a scarf around my mouth. Occasionally people would look, but

One of Calcutta's many thousands of rickshaw pullers. Photo by Dominique Lapierre.

before they realized who I was, I had passed."

The first problem to overcome in pulling a rickshaw is finding the balance. Bigger and fatter passengers make it harder to balance; others sit forward or shift about in the seat. "It is a question of moving your hands up and down the shaft," says Puri. "The other problem is backing up. You cannot just look over your shoulder and move backwards; you have to turn your body and face the passengers and remember how long the rickshaw is. The first time I tried to reverse, my rickshaw was nearly crushed by a bus."

There are 6,000 licensed rickshaw pullers in Calcutta, but it is estimated that at least twice that number operate without a license. (It's said that acquiring a license involves *baksheesh* to the police.) Few pullers own their own rickshaws; most are hired for around 7 rupees a day from someone who may own many. Working an eight-hour day, the puller covers between ten and twenty miles, earning about 79 rupees (about $8) a week.

It is hard and debilitating work. Despite frequent head-to-toe massages with mustard oil, the rickshaw puller's muscles go into spasm from the constant jogging over bad roads, the effort of staying balanced, and sometimes desperate attempts to stop at short notice. Lack of good nourishment and the hazards of pollution make them easy prey to tuberculosis and chest infections that eventually kill many.

Despite the hardships and humiliations of the work, rickshaw pullers have a pride in their calling, and a fierce loyalty to each other that goes beyond competition.

Mainly, though, it is one of the few ways the Calcutta poor can make even a slender living. Hasari Pal calls his rickshaw "a gift of the gods . . . an urban plow with which to make my sweat bear fruit and provide for my children."

Dominique Lapierre,
The City of Joy

Hasari practices with his new rickshaw in the square in the City of Joy.

HASARI
I shall always be grateful.

GHATAK
These days, it's a crop nobody plants.

That evening, Ram and Hasari load Hasari's new rickshaw with the Pals' worldly goods. They are on their way to a new home—in the City of Joy. On arrival, Ram settles them into his own shanty—one room with a sleeping loft—and introduces them to their neighbors.

The family look around their tiny space, hardly able to suppress smiles.

HASARI
Someone has blessed us. A job, a roof, a school. Soon, I'll be able to send money home . . .
(looking at Amrita in delight)
and save some money for my daughter's dowry
(turns to Manooj)
Didn't I tell you I'd find a job?

Hasari practices with the rickshaw under the watchful eye of Ram, racing around the small square in the City of Joy with a heavy sack tied on the rickshaw, to the amusement and delight of all the children. Soon it is time to see if he can really make a living in his new trade on the wealthier streets of Calcutta.

[Rickshaw stand on Park Street]

A schoolgirl in uniform approaches the stand. We see several pullers: Rassoul, Chomotkar, Ramatullah.

SCHOOLGIRL
Rickshaw *wallah!*

RAM
Let Hasari go!

And now we see Hasari—excited, nervous. The pullers turn to Hasari, wish him well. Hasari rubs the moonstone in his ring on the shafts, then touches his heart and his forehead. His heart pounds; ever so politely, he helps the girl into his carriage. She gives him the address of the St. Pius School.

HASARI
I'm sorry, I don't know where that is. You're my very first rider.

SCHOOLGIRL
Really? Well, I hope I bring you luck.

She gives him a sweet smile.

SCHOOLGIRL
That way, and then to the right.

His moment has arrived. He looks at Ram, and thrusts his hips forward, setting off into the insanity of the traffic, eyes flicking left and right. A horn rails at him and a taxi driver tries to run him down, calling and laughing as Hasari jumps in terror.

RAM
(calling after him)
Feed the police!

Other pullers laugh and call after Hasari. As he approaches the first corner, he manages to pull out a rupee and deposit it into the hand of the impassive traffic policeman, and then turn right.

    When they arrive at the school, the girl hands him a slip of paper.

SCHOOLGIRL
This is my home address. Pick me up promptly at seven each morning.

HASARI
Yes, thank you, you can depend on me.

The girl runs into the school yard, met immediately by friends. Hasari looks around at the clean, bustling school, at all the children in their crisp uniforms, and a look of great yearning comes over his face.

"All the cities of the former colonial world have banished them from their roads, as one of the most degrading aspects of man's exploitation of his fellow man. All, except Calcutta, where even today some hundred thousand slave horses harnessed to their rickshaws run up more miles per day than the thirty Boeings and Airbuses of the Indian Airlines. . . . Each day they transport more than one million passengers. . . .

    "With their two large wheels with wooden spokes, their slender bodies and uncurved shafts, rickshaws look like the carriages of our grandmother's day. Invented in Japan at the end of the eighteenth century by a European missionary, their name derives from the Japanese expression *ji riki shaw*, which means literally 'vehicle propelled by man.' The first rickshaws appeared in India around 1800, on the imperial avenues of Simla, the summer capital of the British Indian Empire. Some twenty years later, a few of these vehicles arrived in Calcutta. . . . Faster than the palanquins of olden times and more manageable than hackney carriages, it was not long before rickshaws imposed their presence on the foremost port in Asia."

Dominique Lapierre,
The City of Joy

Ashoka on his motorcycle.

"The goonda, when fully fledged and at the height of his powers, is almost the nastiest customer in Calcutta. A straightforward definition in the dictionary will call him a ruffian, but in Bengal he is a ruffian who is prepared to kill and rob as well as to brawl in back alleys. The police detectives, who study goondas as closely as anyone, are apt to place their origins far away in the time of the East India Company and toss up a quotation from Macaulay to emphasize their point. . . . 'Every servant of a British factor was armed with the power of his master, and his master was armed with the power of the Company. Enormous fortunes were thus rapidly accumulated at Calcutta, while thirty million of human beings were reduced to the last extremity of wretchedness. . . .' When the Indian Mutiny was over and the Company was disbanded . . . the dismissed paiks and lathials promptly began to use on their own account their highly cultivated skills of bullying, blackmail and robbery. . . .

"The goonda's prey can . . . be almost anyone at all, and it is possible that those who suffer most from his terrorism are the very poorest people in Calcutta, who must be bludgeoned or bribed into a political allegiance they will not otherwise follow, or those hundreds of thousands in the city who live in genteel poverty and who offer some source of plunder without the means to defend it."

Geoffrey Moorhouse,
Calcutta

[*A sidewalk restaurant, City of Joy*]
Max, trying to order a hamburger from a bewildered waiter, suddenly spots the shiny gas tank and engine of a familiar-looking motorcycle. It's Ashoka, gunning the engine as a boy puts cassettes into the bag on his bike. Max runs across the road.

MAX
Hey, you! I want my medallion.

Ashoka guns the cycle down the street. Max gives chase and disappears round a corner. Ashoka rides his bike fast through the busy street, weaving his way in and out of traffic. Reaching for the back of the bike, Max trips and falls, abrading his wrist, then continues the pursuit. Ashoka signals to a cop as he rides out of reach.

Joan with Dr. Sunil (left) and City of Joy neighbor Aristotle John.

The cop steps into Max's path; he's badly out of breath.

MAX
Get out of the way! . . . Stop that guy!

COP
May I see your passport, please?

MAX
Passport! He's got my wallet!

COP
Passport, please.

As Max continues to protest, the cop raises his stick to strike. Joan appears and intervenes.

JOAN
Hey, hey, don't do that! He's my friend.

COP
Madam, do you know this fellow?

JOAN
Yes, I do.

COP
But he has no passport.

JOAN
It's all right . . . he's with me.

The cop backs off, still looking suspiciously at Max.

JOAN
Now you owe me three.

Joan looks at Max's wrist, which is bleeding.

JOAN
Don't you think we should have a look at that?

Max follows Joan and her little group of cricket players away down the street.

The lower end of the bustee's main street, with the clinic under construction in the background.

Building a Bustee

"A slum is a place that is allowed to be derelict. A bustee is a place that has been built up with very few resources," notes Roland Joffé. "A slum is about things coming to an end; a bustee is about things starting. The energy is totally different in a bustee."

The need to construct a slum—a bustee, rather—in Calcutta is ironic, since they exist in abundance, springing up wherever the poor can find space to spare. But it would have been impossible to shoot the film in the real City of Joy, a long-established neighborhood whose Hindi name is Anand Nagar. "We could hardly move

people out of their homes," explains Joffé, "so we created our own environment."

The man responsible for creating was became one of Calcutta's great curiosities in the spring of 1991 was Production Designer Roy Walker, who had worked previously with Joffé on *The Killing Fields* and won an Academy Award for his work on *Yentl.*

The set, built on five and a half acres of rented land in Calcutta's docklands, was 500 by 200 feet and contained 60 houses, with another 20 or 30 rooftops and walls for top shots. It was the work of ten English technicians and from 250 to 300 local masons, laborers, painters, and plasterers struggling

Production designer Roy Walker directs the crew.

through the scorching heat and humidity of May and June.

Walker designed the set in London from a three-dimensional model, "to get the idea of perspective." The final construction was very similar, following the same shapes, twists, and bends. "I went for a shape that would be visually interesting for

Workmen finishing a roof.

The real monsoon floods the set in the final stages of construction, July 1990.

the camera and give the director plenty of variety," says Walker. "When we were building, I had a viewfinder with me all the time. Whenever a building was put up, it was done within the camera frame and not for the eye.

"Roland loves long lenses, but on this film he had to change his style a bit. The rooms of the houses are so small, he had to play scenes like a stage, with people acting within a frame. In reality, everything in a bustee is very small. I was impressed with how people managed to cope in that environment. The audience will be aware of people having to stoop and hitting their heads; the Westerners look like giants. It gives everything a reality."

The physical challenge involved in building the set was immense. Walker recalls, "The heat, the rain, the humidity, the noise of tin being battered— there has never been a physical design experience like it. It was more like sculpturing, designing as you went. Boys would literally push the buildings into shape until you said 'stop,' and then put on the roof. Painting was the real secret. Instead of using conventional emulsion, we used powder colors and limewash, and aged it with real soot."

This short-lived "City of Joy" had tea shops, grocery stores, bicycle shops, the self-help clinic and school, cola kiosks, cigarette stalls, and clothing shops. New doors, roofs, and eroded corrugated iron were swapped for old with astonished bustee dwellers. Tattered curtains fluttered from windows; TV aerials sprouted from roofs littered with rubbish and old tires. Water, dyed black to give it a stagnant look, ran in open drains the length of the streets and lay in huge puddles in the squares.

The set was so real that visitors asked, 'How did you manage to buy the houses? Where have all the people gone?' "The only thing lacking," says Shabana Azmi (who plays Kamla), "was the smell."

All photos these pages by the City of Joy *art department.*

A corner near the clinic, showing walls textured with paint and other materials. The bright colors fade quickly in the intense sun.

Joan and Max talk as she wraps up his injured wrist.

[Dispensary, City of Joy]

Joan bandages Max's wrist. Though some information is exchanged here, the scene is also about physical contact between someone with a gentle touch and someone unsure he wants to be touched. Kids are peering at them. Manooj stands boldly right next to Max, watching raptly. Max can also see the young Indian intern, Dr. Sunil Dasgupta, working outside under the awning.

JOAN
If you want these wounds to heal, you really ought to stop abusing yourself.

MAX
Listen to you! Are you just nuts or are you doing penance for some major past sin here?

JOAN
It's not penance, I love it here.

She begins to rewrap his wrist. Manooj leans closer.

JOAN
Of course, it was just a whim in the beginning. I came twice; then I stayed. In the beginning it was really frustrating, trying to convince them not to be so bloody passive—then I realized I was fighting a thousand years of acceptance.

MAX
Maybe you should stop interfering.

JOAN
Maybe I should.

Kamla comes in with a plate of food for Joan, who protests that the woman's kindness will make her fat. Then the dialogue resumes.

MAX
So where do you get the bucks for this set-up?

JOAN
I get a little money from a Swiss organization, and my dear ex-husband sends us money once a month. Jack. He's great. I'm not very good at loving just one person. I get on better when I spread it around a bit.

MAX
Can I ask you something? Don't you feel just a little stupid trying to drill a hole in water like this?

JOAN
Not nearly as stupid as asking someone for a hand and being turned down.

Max very slowly applauds, then stands up and starts to move off. Joan rounds on him.

JOAN
May I be so bold as to ask what you believe in, Max? Do you believe in anything?

MAX
Absolutely, lady. I believe in the Dallas Cowboys, the most consistent winners of the modern era.

Angry, Max goes towards the entrance, to find Manooj and Shambu waiting.

MANOOJ
Do you saw flims, Mr. Max?

MAX
Do I saw flims?

SHAMBU
He is telling you, do you see flims when you were small.

MAX
Did I see flims when I was small? You mean movies, pictures? I used to go three times a week and twice on Saturday. Cartoons . . .Donald Duck . . .

JOAN
Well, you're good with kids anyway.

Max gives her a look—she's gotten to him again—and goes out the doorway. The boys pester Max with questions about Mickey Mouse, etc. Joan shoos them

In the film, Max Lowe quickly develops a rapport with the children of the City of Joy, and it becomes his first link with the community. "Although Max is at first closed off to the adults, he's able to open up quickly with the kids, because it's not threatening—nothing is expected except innocence and naturalness," says Patrick Swayze of his character.

But the actor found that playing the role of "Magic Max," as the kids call him, was far from easy. "Max is expected to entertain the kids with magic tricks, and I trained with a magician back in Los Angeles before production and in Calcutta as well. But what I'd forgotten was that magic was practically invented in India. All these kids know real magicians, maybe even their father or uncle, and they knew all the tricks. If you asked which hand the coin was in, they usually had it wired. So it took a lot of effort to really entertain them and fool them into a performance. I learned a lot about being a good actor by working with those kids."

When he wasn't working on his magic act, Swayze and his wife, Lisa Niemi, taught several of the cast children how to swim in their hotel pool. "After Santu, who plays Shambu, nearly drowned in the pool a couple of times, we realized this was something we could do," Swayze says. "I used to work with my mother, who taught dance and movement to learning-disabled and brain-damaged kids, and we taught a lot of them to swim, too. So I was trained in how to get someone past their fear before they're even aware of it. That was one of the experiences that makes the movie-star stuff seem pretty small by comparison."

away and follows Max out to the porch.

JOAN
Do you know what I've come to think in my old age, Max?

MAX
No idea—you're pretty much an enigma to me.

JOAN
I think in life a person only has three choices.

MAX
And I don't suppose there's any chance you're not going to tell me what they are.

JOAN
To run, to spectate, to commit.

MAX
Very tidy. Simple-minded, but tidy.

JOAN
You're very awfully twisted around, aren't you, Junior?

MAX
Well, one of us sure is.

Dr. Sunil takes his leave.

SUNIL
I'm off, Sister Joan. Nice to meet you, Dr. Lowe.

JOAN
Good night, God bless, Doctor.

They watch him cross the square.

JOAN
Wealthy medical family. Donates his time. Generous young man.

MAX
And clearly not twisted around.

Surya begins to play his zither. We notice Shambu has become a serving boy in the tea shop. As Sunil continues out of the square, Manooj calls out at the sight of Hasari coming in, pulling Ram in his rickshaw.

Hasari can hardly walk. Ram calls out to Surya's customers. Kamla and Amrita are cooking on an open fire bucket.

RAM
Good news! Good news! Hasari has got a regular rider.

Hasari, pretty exhausted, hands over tea cups to Kamla, watched by Amrita.

HASARI
This is for Amrita. We will start a shelf for her.

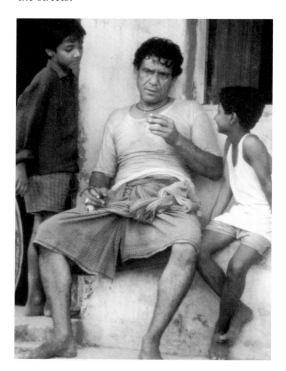

Hasari rests at Ram's hut after a day on the streets.

Mother Teresa. Photo by Symil Kumar Dutt, Camera Press London.

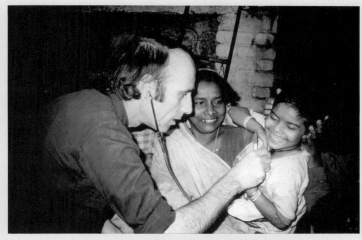

One of the primary models for Stephan Kovalski in The City of Joy examines a child in its mother's arms. Photo by Dominique Lapierre.

Taking It to the Streets: Lives of Service in Calcutta

Calcutta has long been a proving ground for people who are moved to express charity through the works of their own hands. Both Westerners and Indians have responded to the overwhelming needs of its poor and outcast people, who cannot be adequately served by Bengal's social and medical infrastructure. Part of the research done by *City of Joy's* leading actors was to visit and work briefly in the clinics and shelters run by these dedicated workers.

The most celebrated example is Mother Teresa, who in 1946 felt called by God to leave her comfortable teaching post in a Calcutta convent and work among the poorest of the poor. Today her Missionaries of Charity operates close to 300 shelters and several charitable foundations throughout India and the other continents. Its headquarters and soul are still in Calcutta, at Nirmal Hriday (The Place of Pure Heart), Teresa's home for dying destitutes.

The work of Mother Teresa's nuns and their volunteers from around the world also encompasses homes for infants and children, dispensaries and self-help workshops in the leper communities.

More important than physical aid, they bring a message that the suffering poor are valued members of the human community. As Teresa herself says: "I have come more and more to realize that being unwanted is the worst disease that any human being can ever experience. . . ."

Another remarkable caregiver is Dr. Jack Preger, who was similarly called to his work with the poor "who crowd the pavements, disused railway lines, shacks, gutters, the spaces under bridges and flyovers in that 'City of Dreadful Night.'" Preger's activities and views have often put him at risk of imprisonment or deportation by the West Bengal government, yet he is compelled to stay on his path.

When asked about the difficulty of carrying on in impossible conditions, he says, "I am not attached to 'success.' Doing the obvious thing in this appalling situation is enough; and God gives us, in our weakness, victories every day, just to keep us going."

The character of Joan Bethel in the film is based on a Polish priest, Stephan Kovalski, whose story Dominique Lapierre tells in *The City of Joy*. Kovalski, a composite of several dedicated clerics, follows his own call to live among the people of Anand Nagar, and the fruits of his work

Dr. Jack Preger. Photo by Allen Jewhurst.

include a self-help clinic and school similar to the one depicted in the film.

The common experience of these different personalities is that their work brings great fulfillment along with its vast challenge. Mother Teresa's biographer describes the sisters of her order in terms that could apply widely: "Their life is tough and austere by worldly standards . . . yet I never met such delightful, happy women, or such an atmosphere of joy as they create. The poor, Teresa says, deserve not just service and dedication, but also the joy that belongs to human love."

(*The City of Joy*, by Dominique Lapierre; *Something Beautiful for God: Mother Teresa of Calcutta*, by Malcolm Muggeridge; *Destitutes of Calcutta: The Jack Preger Story*, by Frances Meigh)

*The Pals, Max, and other City of Joy residents
share dinner and stories.*

Kamla goes inside. Manooj brings his father some
water. Hasari has got a small packet on his knee.

MANOOJ
What's that?

HASARI
Seeds.

MANOOJ
Why?

HASARI
So we can watch something grow.

Shambu brings Hasari a cup of tea.

SHAMBU
Father, he is a doctor from America. He sees two flims
on Saturday and also Mickey Mouse. Can he eat with
us?

HASARI
Sure.

The boys race over to invite Max to dinner. Afterwards,
they sit around Ram's hut talking, the children planting
seeds under Hasari's directions.

HASARI

Spread them. Sprinkle a little water.
(to Amrita)
When these grow into a flower, I will pluck them and put them in your hair at your wedding. Shambu, go and get some tea.

RAM

At my wedding, I became so frightened, my father gave me something to drink. I went out to piss under a tree and fell asleep. When I awoke, I thought I married the tree. I still love that tree.
(sighs heavily)
If I could pay off the moneylender, I'd go straight back to my village.

MAX

What's a dowry run?

RAM

A heavy burden.

MAX

Why do you bother?

HASARI

It is our duty and honor.

Before Max can respond, everyone's attention is taken by a cry from Shambu, his terrified eyes directing our focus to an amazing sight.

Two lepers: the legless Anouar, bearded with a sharp intelligent, unmarked face, rides on the shoulders of Said, a huge mute. They stop some feet away. Lepers aren't often welcome. Out from behind Said steps Poomina.

ANOUAR

Joan Di!

JOAN

Anouar! What's wrong.

ANOUAR

It's my Meeta.

POOMINA

Joan Di, help my sister!

JOAN

It's all right, Poomina.

ANOUAR

It's Meeta! Her time has come. But something is wrong. There is too much blood. We need Dr. Sunil.

JOAN

Ram, run to Dr. Sunil's house.

SHANTA

Oh no, he's not there. It's his cousin's wedding.

"'I had to leave my village after the death of my father. The poor man had never succeeded in wiping out the family debts that went back to his father and his grandfather. He had mortgaged our land to pay off the interest . . . and when he died I had to borrow even more to give him a proper funeral. Two thousand rupees! . . . I very quickly realized that I would never be able to pay back all that money by staying where I was, especially since, to procure the loan, I had lost our only source of income by mortgaging the next harvest.'"

Ram Chander, in
Dominique Lapierre's
The City of Joy

Anouar arrives at the clinic with news of his wife in labor at the leper colony.

JOAN
How long has she been in labor?

ANOUAR
A long, long time.

JOAN
When did the bleeding start?

POOMINA
Twenty minutes, I think.

ANOUAR
The midwives don't know what to do.

JOAN
What shall we do? I don't know what to do.
(pauses)
Max?

KAMLA
I can come along. I've had three babies.
Max is struggling with himself.

MAX
Do you have any Diazepan?

JOAN
No.

MAX
Sparine?

JOAN
No.

MAX

Do you have anything at this clinic, morphine, anything?

JOAN

No.

MAX

Okay. Get a stethoscope, a suturing kit, a thermometer, hot swabs, compresses . . .

Gets up and follows Joan into clinic.

MAX

Do you have a—a local anaesthetic?

[The leper colony]

The small procession arrives at the leper colony, a cluster of huts near the railroad tracks made of bamboo, plastic sheeting, cloth, wood, and cardboard. A few shadows materialize: lepers, staring silently. Joan and Kamla precede Max inside Meeta's hut.

The only light is the feeble waver of a candle. The blind Meeta lies on a rough mattress on the ground, her ragged sari pulled up to her middle. Her face runs with sweat, her hair is plastered to her face. She sends up a soft, uninterrupted moan.

Max pulls on rubber gloves, begins his examination.

MAX

The baby's breached. Backward. Stethoscope.

He puts a stethoscope in his ears and to Meeta's belly.

MAX

Heartbeat's strong. I'm going to have to turn it. Tell her she has to relax these muscles as much as she can. I'm going to work from the outside and from the inside. I'll be as gentle as I can.

A small group waits outside, trying to determine from the sounds what's happening. Anouar pours *bangla* from a bottle, offers the cup to Hasari. Hasari stares at the cup, doesn't want to be impolite, but more than that, doesn't want to touch the cup. He shakes his head, smiles. Anouar drinks off the *bangla*, pours some more.

Hours pass. There's a sense of real urgency now. Max is drenched and drawn; he's been at this for a long time. Kamla holds Meeta's fingerless palm with her own fine hand. Joan wears the stethoscope now. Max has his hands deep inside Meeta.

"It was medicine that they lacked most. All the American had at his disposal was contained in a small metal trunk: a small quantity of sulphone for the lepers, Ryfomicine for tuberculosis patients, quinine for malaria, a small stock of ointments for skin diseases, and a few vitamins for those children who were suffering most acutely from malnutrition. Finally there were about ten antibiotic tablets for cases of virulent infection. 'There was nothing to brag about,' Max would recount, 'but as Kovalski kept telling anyone prepared to listen, love would make up for all.'"

Dominique Lapierre,
The City of Joy

Long live the newborn child!
We bless you,
That you may live for a long time,
That you may always have good health,
That you may earn lots of money.

Traditional eunuch's blessing for a new baby

JOAN
I can't hear the heartbeat.

We see Poomina's face, her eyes wide, afraid she's going to lose her sister and her sister's baby. Kamla has her hands where Max has placed them on Meeta's belly, working gently each time Max nods at her to massage.

MAX
Massage against me now! Come on, little fellow, don't you die on me! Come on, come on, come on! All right, all right. It's turned! Tell her to push! Push, sweetheart, push!

Max tugs gently.

MAX
I've got the head! Come on, little baby, come on, little baby.

Max gives a last gentle tug and a cry squeezes out of the little piece of life in his hands.

MAX
It's a boy! Hey, little fellow, scream your heart out.

And now there are cries of joy, tears, laughter. Max is fairly overwhelmed. Poomina steps close, a smile on her lovely face, and touches the baby in Max's hands. Kamla stares at Max, helplessly drawn through this experience to him.

[Nizamudhin Lane, City of Joy]
The weary group walks home at dawn. Max catches Hasari looking at him curiously.

MAX
Your wife was great. She should be a nurse.

A little smile comes over Kamla's face. No one's ever paid her that kind of compliment. She flicks her eyes guiltily at Hasari, who's taken aback by the suggestion.

HASARI
Thank you for your kind words. I was dearly blessed to marry her.

And he smoothly changes the subject.

HASARI
You have birthed many babies?

MAX
Not for a long time.

Max turns inward, closed off to further questions. They walk on a moment. Back at the dispensary, Joan suddenly grasps Max's hand.

JOAN
Max, you can see how desperately we need a doctor, full-time. Just give us a couple of months.

He recoils from her touch and from the pressure.

MAX
I'm sorry. Maybe you can be a saint, Sister Joan, but I just don't have it in me.

JOAN
So what are you going to be when you grow up, Doctor?

MAX
Listen, don't do that, lady! Don't patronize me because you're on some kind of goddammned do-gooder trip!

JOAN
Don't you stick your chest out at me, I'll smack you upside the head!

Hasari and Kamla watch this, stupefied.

Like some of the other actors, Swayze spent time volunteering in Calcutta's charitable institutions. "The first day I got there, Roland put me in a car and took me to Mother Teresa's home for the dying," he recalls. He also worked in a hospital for lepers outside Calcutta and in Dr. Jack Preger's street clinic. He vividly recalls an experience that parallels Max Lowe's in the film, of being thrown into a medical emergency with desperately slim resources.

"A little boy came in who'd had his arm bandaged for third-degree burns, and because people so often don't get any follow-up care, the bandages had grown right into his flesh. It was my job to get them off, irrigating with a syringe and cutting the dead flesh away. My Swiss Army knife was the best and sharpest tool available."

Swayze had to stop volunteering after a few weeks because "Roland and I found that these experiences were opening me up too fast for the character of Max, who has to stay in a cynical, self-indulgent mood for much of the movie. Also, the shooting schedule became too heavy for a while. But after I moved into the stage where Max becomes something resembling a whole human being, I started working in the clinics again."

Kamla, Hasari, Joan, and Max return to the clinic after their long night.

MAX

You are so goddamned self-righteous! I don't even feel good about what we did back there. Another little mouth to feed in this cesspool of a country!

JOAN

Feel good! Who the hell cares if you feel good! What makes you so special! You're just a person like the rest of us, doing the best you can to take care of yourself—and not doing any too bloody well at it, as far as I can see!

MAX

Don't talk like you think you know me, lady!

JOAN

Look, you need help. Don't be a coward—ask for it! *(She heads for the door.)*

Roland Joffé:
The Inquiring Mind
Behind the Lens

Director Roland Joffé had just completed work on *The Mission* when he read an early proof of Dominique Lapierre's *The City of Joy*. Possessed immediately by the determination to turn it into a film, he faced the first of many challenges: how to create a coherent screen drama from the many-stranded texture of Lapierre's tapestry of Calcutta.

He could see that among the 50 or 60 characters in the book, Hasari Pal stood out. "I thought there was something of the everyman about him, this man who comes to Calcutta as a refugee with nothing but his family and has to earn their living by pulling people around in a rickshaw. Counterpoise Hasari against a Westerner, Max Lowe, a man in a crisis, a man who has come to a full stop, and a wealth of contrasts begins to open up.

"An Indian proverb says that of the five most important people in your life, the most important will be your teacher. If you ever know who he is, you are lucky. Hasari and Max are both lucky to find each other.

"For Hasari, to get through every single day of his life is a real victory, but to break the chains that bind him to the men who demand his allegiance (like Ashoka and the Godfather), he needs the interaction with someone who has different view of life. For Max, coming to terms with a city of survivors becomes a way of finding the strength to beat his personal devils.

"Film, like nineteenth-century novels, should be incredibly rich and diverse, not afraid of scale and in favor of human beings, not divided and cynical as so much art has been since World War II. But you have to

Roland Joffé and Camera Operator Mike Roberts confer on a street shot.

start with the premise that a film is closer to a poem than to a novel. The structure of a film—the setting of one image against another—is very close to the structure of poetry. It's the way you put those images together that creates something with aspects of reality."

The actors in *City of Joy* appreciated the amount of give-and-take Joffé encouraged in developing their characters, the fluid nature of their collaboration. Joffé's Director of Photography, Peter Biziou, noted the same tendency: "Roland would tend to let all the elements work in front of him and find his way with them."

He is a director who likes to improvise, and this can give the technicians problems. "Improvisation can be exasperating but it is also exciting," Biziou adds. "Although Roland will demand and push to get things done, he knows that sometimes it doesn't work, and you have to stop pushing."

The need for both flexibility and precision often resulted in

many takes of a scene. "They were always for good reasons," says Biziou. "Roland does not waste time with unimportant details, and the number of takes related to the complexity of the shots. Also, we were dealing with many nonprofessionals, moving the camera in a particularly brave way, and being very precise with our timing. Each shot had an orchestration to it. The shots may look simple but it took a lot to make them work."

"Directing is the art of flowing with the question," says Joffé. "I absorb like a sponge everything I can. In that way one finds images that convey an essence—the meaning that lies behind the everyday—and that is all a film can do.

"I could never work by saying that I have answers to everything. All I can say is that I have an inquiring mind and I relish questions. It doesn't matter to me if a film ends on a question mark; often it should. I love the audience to go out of a film still engaged in the creative process."

Have a pleasant journey home, Max. Goodbye and God bless.

Joan goes inside, leaving a furious Max and a most uncomfortable Kamla and Hasari. Someone has to speak. Hasari approaches him hesitantly.

HASARI
Mr. Max, I . . . I think you have a good heart.

Max walks off the verandah, passing Kamla, who turns.

KAMLA
Thank you for allowing me to be of use.

This is too much. Max bolts off down the lane as fast as he can run.

PART II

✤ Blood, Sweat, and Fear ✤

✤ Blood, Sweat, and Fear ✤

Preceding page: *Hasari takes his schoolgirl rider and her mother to the bridal shop.*

[Green Acres Hotel]

The day is heating up and people are starting to sweat. Max is in the foyer, leaning over the reception desk trying not to shout into the telephone. The manageress is watching him as she walks down the stairs and around the back of her reception desk.

MAX

I can't understand how it takes three weeks to transfer a couple of hundred dollars. . . . I just gave it to you—one one zero zero one sixty two. . . . Two. *Dos.* How do I know my visa . . . Hello?

Puts the phone back, and collects his ticket and notebook.

MAX

No dinero, no bucks, not for three weeks. This is turning into a bad dream.

MANAGERESS

Max, the bill. I need your plane ticket.

MAX

My plane ticket?

MANAGERESS

A little guarantee.

MAX
(mimicking her)

A little guarantee. A face like this, and you don't trust me?

MANAGERESS

It's not a question of trust, Max. The government needs this foreign exchange.

MAX

Oh, it's the government's fault.

MANAGERESS

And my husband is a very strict man.

MAX

And I suppose we have to tell your husband.

The manageress nods her head, still smiling.

MAX

And there's no other way out of this country . . . hunchback camel, rickshaw, burro?

MANAGERESS

Not until your bill has been paid.

Max hands over his ticket.

MAX

There. Please don't lose it.

He picks a single rose from a nearby basket, presents it with a flourish to the entranced manageress, and goes.

[The square, City of Joy]
An argument is in process. Several lepers from the colony have come to the dispensary to be treated, and some of the locals are objecting to their presence.

Said carries Anouar from the leper colony to the clinic to see Max.

Nabil Shaban as Anouar

Anouar, a leader of the leper community in City of Joy, is played by disabled actor Nabil Shaban. Shaban overcame considerable negative advice to found an acting company for the disabled in England, and has played a variety of leading roles in London and provincial theaters.

When first offered the role of Anouar, Shaban felt that it should go to a real leper. Swayed by the argument that Indian crews might resist working with a main character who was a leper, he then went to work on Roland Joffé to strengthen and sharpen his character. Together they shaped Anouar into a true leader who is argumentative without losing his humor.

"When I first met Nabil," recalls Joffé, "he was ferociously independent, enormously prickly. He passionately wanted to do the film, told me exactly how he felt, and didn't let me get a word in. I realized he had survived by fighting back, and this fitted with one of the strong themes of the film: that we should be very wary of compassion. It can imply contempt, as if saying, 'Poor thing, he's not really a human being.'

"Nabil quite rightly didn't want to be treated that way. The people in the film learn to fight back; the leper gains his self-respect. In that way, they don't feel dejected and subhuman; they are just humans desperately battling to sort out their problems, as we all are. That was the spirit of the book, and I think Nabil embodied it in his wit and humor and courage."

"As far as I was concerned," says Shaban, "playing this part was not just saying something on behalf of lepers, but on the part of disabled people. I know that seeing me as Anouar will make an impact in terms of disabled people."

Others defend their right to be there, saying they are no danger. Sunil tells them leprosy is not contagious but many are unmoved.

Joan comes out of a hut. Anouar, in Said's arms, appears from the alleyway.

JOAN
Anouar!

ANOUAR
Joan Di, tell us. Dr. Lowe was telling us that many of us could be helped. All it would take is money for medication.
(holds out a leather sack of coins)
Please, would you buy us the medication?

JOAN
Anouar, it'd cost a fortune.

ANOUAR
As we cannot come here to receive it, perhaps Dr. Lowe would come to us occasionally.

JOAN
Dr. Lowe is not part of this endeavor, Anouar; there is only his cherished memory.

ANOUAR

Then perhaps I am on the moon, because I am having visions.

Anouar is smiling, and his focus is up the lane. Joan turns to look. Max heading toward us, carrying a large value pack of bar soaps.

MAX

Good morning! Good morning! Helluva morning! You practicing medicine without a license, Sister Joan?

Joan greets him, gives him a hug.

JOAN

Oh God, Junior, you're great! I do love to be surprised.

Max backs away slightly.

MAX

Don't get carried away. I'm just here to get you guys organized.

JOAN

But you showed up. What made you change your mind?

MAX

I had a religious experience.

JOAN

Sure, and I'm a bathing beauty.

They walk on toward the clinic.

MAX

Actually, I am temporarily deprived of my plane ticket.

Max and Joan strike a deal.

They enter the clinic, negotiating how long Max will stay. He offers a few weeks; she counters with six months; they end up agreeing on nine weeks.

MAX

Okay, sit down. Write. We need detailed case histories . . . we need an IV . . . we need a truckload of broad spectrum antibiotic, pain killers, basic vaccines . . .

JOAN

Oh God, save me from knights in shining armor!

A little while later, Max moves over to Ram's hut. Greeting Hasari and Kamla, he asks her to act as his assistant at the clinic, then belatedly turns to Hasari and asks his permission. Both agree: Kamla eagerly, Hasari a bit cautiously.

Life in the City of Joy resumes its familiar rhythm, with a few changes. Max and Kamla work every day in the dispensary, with frequent trips to the leper colony, whose residents are still shunned by even the slum dwellers.

Hasari spends the days at his rickshaw, coming to know the city better, twice each day picking up and returning home his regular passenger from school. One day, the girl's mother accompanies her, and they take a different route: to an exclusive bridal shop where they are to choose her wedding sari.

SCHOOLGIRL
You must remember this shop, Hasari, when it's your daughter's time. This is the nicest in the city.

The mother gives the girl a withering look and hustles her into the shop. Hasari can just barely hear.

MOTHER
Don't embarrass him like that. How's he ever going to buy anything here?

Hasari watches from outside, a look of determination coming over his face.

One day Meeta brings her new baby to the clinic for a checkup. Max is drenched and dirty; Meeta in a bright sari and a lot of bracelets. Kamla assists. Poomina clings to the wall. Max finishes with an old patient.

MAX
Not two a day. One every two days.

JOAN
Never mind, Junior, only another four hours.

MAX
Okay, little fella. Let's check you out. How much does he weigh?

KAMLA
One and a half kilos.

MAX
This baby's not gaining weight.
(*addresses Meeta*)
Are you giving him the extra milk we gave you?

Kamla translates for Meeta. Meeta hedges.

KAMLA
Some. Not all.

JOAN
She's probably selling it.

MAX
Selling it!

Frightened by the tone of Max's voice, Meeta recoils. Sunil slips in quickly, goes to the shelf of now carefully catalogued medication.

"The conversion of souls in any orthodox sense . . . is rather beside the point Mother Teresa is trying to make.

"The point is clear enough in the shed at Nirmal Hriday, where people are dying in a scrap of dignity, surrounded by much care and attention; it is evident out at Dhapa, where the lepers are encouraged to struggle on with their mutilations. . . . At the dispensary just down the road from the convent, the point seems to be that a lot of sick people are being inoculated, cajoled into taking medicines of which they may be suspicious, occasionally scolded for failing to take pills as prescribed, because that is what you do if you have some medical training and a few resources and when you are always confronted with sick people. . . . At the orphanage the point of the exercise appears to be that if you hear the mew of a kitten upon a garbage heap one day and, on investigating, discover that it is not a kitten but a very new baby shaped and sized like a wizened rat, you bring it back and try to rear it out of pre-natal malnutrition so that it will be strong enough to face existence in Calcutta. . . ."

Geoffrey Moorhouse,
Calcutta

Max examines Meeta's baby.

JOAN
She has to pay rent.

MAX
On that dump?

JOAN
Yeah. Now Poomina's going to school, somebody's got to pay the rent. That's how it works round here.

POOMINA
I am not like in school to be in. I will go back to my work. I'll earn money.

Meeta chips in her bit in Hindi. Max calls a halt.

MAX
Whoa, whoa! We have the technology, okay?
(goes and gets two cans of milk)
This is extra milk for the baby—and this is extra extra milk for the rent. It's simple . . . give it to the kid, or I'll kill you.

Kamla translates to Meeta, who thanks Max shyly. Max turns to Poomina.

MAX
You, little lady, will stay in school. Don't look at me like that.

"Hindi, the great lingua franca of modern India, now spoken by nearly a quarter of a billion people, was understood by the majority of the occupants of the City of Joy. It was one of twenty or thirty languages used in the slum; others were Bengali, Urdu, Tamil, Malayalam, Punjabi, and numerous dialects."

Dominique Lapierre,
The City of Joy

Kamla glances at Joan, both pleased Max has learned something. Sunil glances over and smiles, then ducks back out. At this point, the baby pees all over Max, who starts laughing.

MAX
Gonna be a fireman when he grows up. I get no respect.

Still, life in the City of Joy remains a daily struggle, and Max's presence does not bring unalloyed joy. On more than one night, Hasari arrives home exhausted to find dirty plates in the house, or supper cooked by one of the children and lacking in salt. These lapses in housekeeping are because Kamla is busy with Max at the clinic.

Another ongoing problem is the difficulty of treating people in the distant leper colony, still denied access to the clinic.

One night Hasari arrives home, aching. Finds Shambu struggling to cook supper. Shambu smiles proudly; Hasari isn't pleased.

Max and Kamla drag into the square, sweaty, whipped at the end of another long day. Margareta and Joan release the children from school. They charge into the square.

The City of Joy *set from above.*

Hasari is outside Ram's hut, cleaning his rickshaw. Max and Kamla greet him. His greeting is less than warm. Joan joins them with Manooj and Amrita.

JOAN
Hasari, you've got three fine potential scholars here.
(indicates Manooj)
This one will be ready for a proper school in another couple of years.

HASARI
It's more than a father could hope.

MAX
Fifteen years from now: Dallas, Texas, Dr. Manooj Pal, in association with Dr. Maxwell Lowe.
(to Joan)
Joan, we can't keep going out to that leper colony. We're wasting, what, two hours a day walking.

Poomina runs into their midst now and shoves an envelope into Joan's hand.

MAX
Hey, where were you today, miss? You should be in school!

Joan opens the letter resignedly.

JOAN
I know who this is from.

[The Zamindar's Throne Room]
Music of days gone by plays on an old radio. Mr. Ghatak, the Godfather, leads Joan and Max from the verandah into a big room, passing a television showing a heart transplant film, and the paper-stacked billiards table.

JOAN
Now, Mr. Ghatak, I understand the rent should go up if we have larger quarters, but I don't see why we have to pay more protection.

GHATAK
More people, more problems. Strangers. If I don't charge you, what will I tell others?

JOAN
But we can't afford it!

GHATAK
If you can expand, you can afford to pay more.

MAX
Excuse me, sir. This is a free clinic, not a drinking den.

The Godfather slowly looks him up and down.

Hasari shows his displeasure at Kamla's absence.

A fact of life in Calcutta is "the extortion business conducted by the Mafia, with the cooperation of certain authorities. It was a strictly indigenous 'Mafia' which had no reason to envy its famous Italo-American model. . . .

"Every time a handful of refugees stopped somewhere to set up some kind of shanty, the Mafia representative would turn up armed with a *bona fide* demolition order issued by the city's authorities. The squatters then found themselves confronted with a choice between paying regular rent or purchasing the plot. . . . The bloodsuckers did not, however, confine their racket merely to collecting rents and other 'residential taxes.' Their control extended, in fact, to all aspects of life in the slum. Being the only local authority, the Mafia set itself up as the 'protector' of the population. In a way its claim was true . . . [but] Anyone who dared to question the legitimacy of this underground power was punished without mercy."

Dominique Lapierre,
The City of Joy

Ghatak tells Max and Joan his version of the facts of life in Calcutta.

GHATAK

You are from a rich country, doctor. To you, money is a piece of paper to buy something. For me it is a wall. A beautiful wall. A protecting wall. A wall that separates me from the degradation on the other side. This wall is my achievement, Miss Bethel. I am proud of it. And what you fail to understand is that those poor souls on the other side are also proud of it. Do you understand?

MAX

Oh, yes.

GHATAK

Please be seated.

In Hindi, he sends a man outside for something. Joan and Max take their seats. Out of the corner of his eye, Max sees Ashoka lurking in the dark hallway. Ashoka slowly raises Max's medallion, which hangs around his neck, and puts it in his mouth. Max looks back at the Godfather, who addresses Joan.

GHATAK

So, you wish to begin the treatment of lepers. Your neighbors are simple, not educated. They won't tolerate lepers.

JOAN

They'll change.

Ghatak gives her a look part derisory, part admiring.

GHATAK
Change! You are a romantic, Miss Bethel. I've learned not to trust those who say they do things for the benefit of others.

The thug Ghatak sent outside returns with a chicken.

GHATAK
Dear doctor, a man can be tamed by having an abundance or by having nothing. Who is rebellious? Who is disobedient? Those who have only a little. So if there is not enough for all, it is best that the people have nothing.

Ghatak takes the chicken and puts it on the table.

GHATAK
My children bask in the light of my strength. It brings stability. But I burden my children carefully, kindly . . . reading their faces . . . adding to their burdens in tiny increments.

Ghatak takes a small weight from the desk and puts it on the chicken's back, then takes away his hands. The chicken stands stock still, perfectly controlled by the addition of just the right weight. Joan and Max, needless to say, are raptly attentive.

GHATAK
So—tranquility and an end to pointless aggression.

He looks at the immobilized chicken, at his guests, turns his palms up, smiles, and takes up a plate of pastries. He holds the plate out to Joan, who politely takes one.

GHATAK
You really ought to give up thinking, Doctor. Learn to enjoy yourself. I'm sure we can provide the means to remove those clouds from your forehead.

He nods toward the door, where we saw Poomina, and holds the plate of pastries out to Max. Max erupts.

MAX
Don't offer me candy. What are you trying to do, bribe me?

The thugs are instantly on the alert as Max smacks the plate out of Ghatak's hand, sending it crashing across the desk, sending the chicken flying. The Goonda and the thugs are about to pounce as Max, like an uncaged animal, looks for an exit. The chicken shrieks and bounds.

   Fascinated, Ghatak lifts a hand to stop his men from landing on Max. Joan hustles him out of the house as fast as she can.

✤

Ashoka watches the proceedings closely.

Outcasts

Hindu society is built on caste. At the top is the Brahmin, at the bottom, the untouchable Harijan, and beyond this ordered world are the lepers, reviled and unwanted by everyone. There are between 30,000 and 40,000 victims of leprosy in Calcutta. Most hospitals will not treat them, and Mother Teresa's nuns are among the very few willing to care for them.

The sisters of her Missionaries of Charity order patrol the most neglected areas of Calcutta in mobile clinics to bring aid to those who would otherwise not venture to her houses.

This applies especially to lepers, who are not welcome outside the wretched ghettos where they cluster by the hundreds. Writes Dominique Lapierre: "The horror and fear inspired by disfigured faces, hands and feet reduced to stumps, and wounds at times infested with vermin, condemned the lepers of Anand Nagar to total segregation. Although they were free to go about the slum, an unspoken code forbade them to enter the houses or compounds of the healthy."

Nabil Shaban, who plays the legless leper Anouar in the film, spoke with one of the dedicated priests who care for Calcutta's lepers. "I learned that . . . the worst effects of the disease are sociological. They become outcasts, no matter what level of society they come from. They are thrown out of their jobs, and their families disown them."

This point is made by Mother Teresa herself: "Among the lepers there are many well-educated people, many rich and capable people. But owing to the disease they have been thrown out of society . . . very often even their own children do not want to see them any more. . . ."

The lot of Calcutta's lepers is slowly improving, due to the

Dominique Lapierre and his wife at the home for leper children his royalties help to sponsor. Photo by Baldev/Sygma.

efforts of those such as Teresa and the growing realization among lepers that their disease is treatable. Author Lapierre is instrumental in this effort, donating large sums each year from his royalties and outside donations to a home for the children of lepers. And Mother Teresa's organization has set up self-help workshops for those lepers well enough to work—a huge step in giving them back their self-respect.

Roland Joffé made a visit to one such self-help center during the filming. "The leper colony was basically four or five buildings along the railroad line, shacks converted to workshops, the trains whistling past. Inside, you see these people with their maimed hands working quite complicated looms, making robes for Mother Teresa's nuns all around the world, as well as other things.

"Even today lepers in India feel they're valueless. One man I met, a respectable post office employee, became an instant outcast when he found he had leprosy; thrown off his job and out of his home. The work is giving them their dignity back.

If a man or a woman can work, contribute something, they feel they're worth something.

"One image that stays with me from walking through the workshop is of young girl who was having wounds on her leg treated. They were worm holes—she'd been eaten by maggots. She was fourteen now; eight when her family found out about her leprosy. They were so horrified they locked her in cupboard, where she'd spent all her time, with scraps of food thrown to her, being eaten by maggots who moved from the food to her body.

"But now she was being cured, made whole. . . . As a nun brushed her hair, probably for the first time in her life, her face had the most extraordinary expression, the faintest glimmer of enjoyment at being touched. It struck me that the act of not touching a leper is an act of brutality, because it confirms that they're not there. Touch is the most direct affirmation that we exist. This need for human physical contact is clearly so important in other situations, too, such as for AIDS patients."

[Tea shop, City of Joy]
Max sits among the City of Joy residents.

CHOMOTKAR
You must admit, at least the Godfather is civilized, but this son is vicious. You don't know, sir. Remember the elections, the molotov cocktails, the blows with iron bars. They'll throw us out. We won't find anyone else to rent to us. Joan Di, we'll have to agree to pay whatever they want.

MEHBOUB
Chomotkar's right. These people with power have no conscience. They will kill us. We must pay.

ASHISH
Dr. Sunil, what do you have to say?

SUNIL
I think we must try to break the Godfather's hold on us.

This is startling, and is met with a babble of cautious agreement and dispute.

SUNIL
This is exactly what I'm saying. I think we must be cautious, and this may not be the most appropriate time!

The City of Joy community meets to debate the Godfather's demand for more protection money.

"Fishes can't afford to live on bad terms with the crocodiles in the pool."

Indian rural proverb

MAX
Look, if you want to change things, you gotta risk. How do you proceed with caution against someone who considers you a chicken with a weight around his neck? You compromise with these people, they will kill you.

Kamla listens on the outskirts of the gathering.

JOAN
You can stand up to them. We live here. We can't do that.

MAX
You stand up to them and they will back down, I guarantee it. You compromise with these guys, they'll eat you alive.

SUNIL
Please, this is not an American gangster TV show, Max!

JOAN
Max, we have to be careful . . . this is a self-help society.

MAX
So help yourself.

JOAN
We're not getting swept into your thing!

MAX
I take offense at that, Saint Joan.

JOAN
Yes, well, I'm sorry you're so sensitive, but this is too important to piss about.

SUNIL
It's so hard to know when to trust you, you're angry at everything.

MAX
You ain't seen nothin' yet!

The debate goes on. Finally Hasari's opinion is asked. He considers his words carefully.

HASARI
He has given me a job, and I have been eating his salt. It is difficult . . . I don't know what to say. Joan Di, you understand.

MAX
I don't believe you people. You're acting like sheep! You bow your heads, you put up with this, he will rule you for the rest of your life!

People shout their opinions once again. Anouar strikes an iron bar to quiet the crowd.

KAMLA
May I be permitted to speak?

Shabana Azmi as Kamla

Described by the legendary Satyajit Ray as "one of the finest dramatic actresses of our country," Shabana Azmi gives a many-layered performance as Kamla, Hasari Pal's wife, who discovers untapped strengths when recruited as a nurse by Dr. Max Lowe.

The daughter of a famous Urdu poet and a stage actress, Azmi studied psychology in college before beginning to work in theater and film. She has appeared in more than 100 films in India and has won every major acting award her country can bestow. In 1988 she earned high praise for her performance in *Madame Sousatzka,* her first film in English. She has served on the juries of several international film festivals and been honored with a retrospective of her films at the Pompidou

Center in Paris.

Alongside her acting career, Azmi is active in civil liberties issues in India. A founding member of an organization to protect the slum dwellers of Bombay, she is also chairwoman of the Anti-Dowry Action Committee in Bombay, and is associated with two women's groups seeking to protect uneducated rural women from exploitation. For her social contributions she was given—along with Mother Teresa and 16 other women— the International Human Rights Award by President Mitterrand of France in 1986.

Roland Joffé says of her: "Shabana is politically very astute and aware. She understands what it is to be an Indian woman, and her understanding blends into the character. . . . There is a rock inside Shabana as well as external beauty."

The most challenging part of her role, Azmi relates, was portraying Kamla's shyness, "because as a person shyness is not one of my virtues. Roland suggested that the shyness came from her being deeply bound by tradition. So she plays the role of wife and mother—but she should be played as if she has a volcano inside her that must be held back. When she comes in contact with the doctor and the clinic, she can realize her own self-esteem."

A small uproar again breaks out, quieting to let Kamla speak.

KAMLA
It is only because this is our home now. We have never known such friends. I think the Godfather is strong and could kill us. But we must choose. Dr. Max is only trying to be helpful. I think we should support him. I think we should stand up.

CHOMOTKAR
But who is going to lend us the space?

SURYA
Well, I have a property which I could rent, for two hundred and fifty rupees a month. But . . . not a rupee less.

And so it is settled. Soon there will be a new clinic and school. The whole community sets to work transforming Surya's ramshackle building and clearing the courtyard outside. Two cows are shooed out of the building. Debris is torn out, hurled into a pile in the street. Anouar is kept very busy supervising the operation.

Ashoka waylays Hasari and the children on a side street.

[The Godfather's bedroom]
Ghatak sitting in a chair, the TV close, a heart operating running. Ashoka and the Goonda are close by.

ASHOKA
Those *goras* are going to open a new clinic on someone else's property. They are not going to pay protection. I think the doctor must go.

GHATAK
How many times does a heart beat in a man's lifetime?

Ashoka doesn't answer.

GHATAK
I've calculated it. Two billion times.

ASHOKA
The nurse is okay. The doctor, the American, must go now.

Ghatak suddenly slaps his son hard.

GHATAK
I am ill. I am sick. I don't want to hear of it.
(moderating his tone as Ashoka cringes away)
Infant. Are they going to bring in lepers, heh?

ASHOKA
Yes.

GHATAK
Good. We will let them climb well out on the branch—
then we'll cut it off.

[A side street]
Hasari rounds a corner with the rickshaw, the three kids
sitting in it. A motorcycle with Ashoka and the Goonda
astride swerves in front of Hasari, forcing him to jam to
a stop, jolting the kids. Ashoka dismounts and takes
Hasari by the ear.

ASHOKA
Who gives you your livelihood?

HASARI
Your father, Babu.

ASHOKA
Remember: Loyalty.

He slaps Hasari's face, remounts the bike, and roars off.
Hasari looks at his children, ashamed to have been
cowed. Manooj fixes his father with a hard look.

[Ram's hut]
Hasari and Kamla are in the sleeping loft, Hasari sitting
up, worrying.

HASARI
The Godfather has made our life here possible. We
shouldn't anger him.

KAMLA
I think we can trust Max Daddah. It was Dr. Max who
helped you get your rickshaw.

Hasari is feeling very vulnerable, threatened, confused.
He gazes intensely at Kamla, touches her face. The
touching leads to lovemaking.

*Work on the new clinic continues. Roof tiles are laid, windows are
caulked. Equipment and furnishings from the old clinic are being
moved from the square down here.*

Max and Kamla do one of those dances where two
people with arms loaded try to go around each other.
Finally, he says he'll stand still and she should go
around him. They both laugh.
    In an upstairs room, Max and Hasari maneuver a bed
into position.

MAX
What are you doing?

O, my heart,
Let us go then
On a promenade
To the grove
Of Krishna's love.
The breeze
Of joy
Will calm
Your life.

In that woodland
Eternally bloom
Five scented flowers.
Their fragrance
Will enchant
Your life and soul,
Giving them
Sovereign dignity. . . .

**The Baul poet Ananta,
from *Songs of the Bards
of Bengal***

Indian Actors in a Western Film

The cast of *City of Joy* features some of India's finest actors, including Om Puri, who plays Hasari Pal, Shabana Azmi in the role of his wife, Kamla, and Art Malik as the gangster Ashoka. Nearly all of the remaining 40 cast members are Indian actors based in Calcutta, Delhi, and Bombay.

"Casting and working with the Indian actors was a wonderful experience," says Roland Joffé. "They were my information flow. I had to keep learning about India, and the actors could teach me."

Casting Director Priscilla John, who worked on both *Jewel in the Crown* and *A Passage to India*, spent the better part of a year going back and forth to India searching out qualified actors for *City of Joy*. "The characters had to speak English," she says, "but had to be fundamentally Indian. There's a wealth of acting talent in India, especially in Calcutta, where everyone really loves theater in the purist sense."

India does not have a casting system like those in the U.S. or England, and actors are not represented by agents. Therefore John had to do a lot of legwork, viewing films and theater and visiting actors at their homes. Another problem was the availability of stars like Om Puri and Shabana Azmi. Indian actors commonly make up to 30 films at once. "The schedules of the big stars are so full it was impossible for them to give us a week, let alone 15 weeks," notes John. "Om and Shabana had to clear their schedules for us, which was quite difficult."

Once the cast was assembled, the filmmakers faced the challenge of forging them into a unified ensemble, despite cultural

barriers. One technique they used was a series of pre-shooting workshops led by writer and director Donald Mackechnie "My job was to give Roland a life in the bustee, to build a family, try to create emotional fields around the lives of the workshop actors," Mackechnie says.

Joffé recalls, "When I wanted to make the film, I was warned, 'You'll never understand Indian culture; nobody will work together; the gaps are too big; you'll patronize them. My reaction was that if I obeyed these rules—if the world did—we'd never make any progress. It meant admitting there was an uncrossable divide. I recognized that there was a divide but thought it was crossable.

"So I went back to basics. It seemed to me that all human beings have the same deep questions: How to cope with love and its absence, how to find meaning, what do loyalty and faithfulness mean. These are universal issues; whether I worked with the Waunana Indians in Columbia or with Cambodians in Thailand, I found that basically we shared

the same questions.

"It occurred to me that we can see culture as a series of answers people find to cope with these questions, to provide meaning and structure for their lives. Other peoples' answers are often indecipherable, so I decided to abandon answers and go in with the questions.

"In the workshops I tried to elicit the actors' answers to some very basic questions—not directly but through improvisation and other subtle ways, getting them and us to see the differences and similarities in our answers. By concentrating on the similarities while acknowledging the differences, we began to forge links. I've always tried to focus on the areas where we connect rather than where we disconnect."

When filming in different cultures, it is important to accommodate the script dialogue to the rhythms of the native language. Joffé was particularly skillful at this, says Priscilla John, encouraging the Indian actors—especially the children—to say the words in their own way.

HASARI
(breathing hard)
Just a little breath.

MAX
I thought you were the farmer.

HASARI
Doctor Max, will this be your room?

MAX
No, no, it's Joan Di's room. Is that a smile? I knew it.

HASARI
Doctor Max, I really didn't think all this would work,
but it has. Now all you need is an Indian bride.

MAX
And you're going to pick her! Get out of town!

*On the day of the new clinic's opening, Joan makes a little speech,
welcoming one and all. A hand-lettered banner is ceremoniously
raised amid noisy celebration. All who took part in the building feel
a surge of pride and accomplishment.*

*The community celebrates the opening of the
new clinic and school.*

Max's sightseeing trip with Anouar and Meeta is interrupted by the sight of demonstrators near the clinic.

The wheel of life takes another turn. Hasari, arriving one day with the rickshaw to take Manooj and Amrita home from the workshop where they are employed, notices a handsome boy who catches Amrita's eye as they leave. Amrita is sweetly embarrassed to find her father staring at her. He is reminded again of his parental obligations.

A letter arrives for Max at the Green Acres Hotel one morning, offering him a job back home. Strangely enough, he seems to have mixed feelings about it.

[Green Acres Hotel]
Max is interrupted in reading his letter by the unexpected arrival of Anouar and Meeta in Hasari's rickshaw.

MAX
Oh my god, lepers!
(to the manageress)
Put that in my box, please. There goes the neighborhood.

ANOUAR
Sssshhh, you barbarian! Please, we're trying not to be lepers!

MAX

Ahh, of course, I didn't get the concept—not lepers. You had me fooled.

ANOUAR

We've come to take you to the clinic in grand style on this special day.

MAX

Great, let's go!

Max climbs aboard the rickshaw. They pull out onto the street.

ANOUAR

Meeta's very excited by this ride through Calcutta. You see, she's never been sightseeing before.

Meeta, of course, is blind. The men laugh.

MAX

You're incorrigible, Anouar.

ANOUAR

Yes, yes, I know, I am encourageable.

MAX

That's not what I said.

[Riverbank and side street]
Margareta, Manooj, Shambu, and several other kids carry water on their heads toward the City of Joy. Poomina is at the end of the line. Suddenly, one of Ashoka's thugs appears and whispers to Poomina. She glances after Margareta and the others, who are turning a corner and steps into a side street, where Ashoka waits.

ASHOKA

You like the clinic?

Ashoka takes his revenge on Poomina for her desertion.

(she nods, whimpers)
And they like you?
(she nods again)
And they love your smile, don't they?

She's fearful, doesn't respond. He grabs her, the water pitcher crashes to the ground. He puts his razor blade into her mouth and lays her face open on both sides.

As the party in the rickshaw approaches the clinic, it's clear that something is wrong. A shouting crowd waves placards protesting the presence of lepers at the clinic, whipped to a frenzy by Ashoka's gang.

Joan confronts the Goonda at the clinic gate, but is overwhelmed as the mob storms in. The violence quickly escalates as Max, Joan, and Kamla try to herd their patients inside.

Kamla urges the lepers forward but is stopped by a blow from the Goonda's stick across her shoulders, knocking her to the ground. Hasari bolts for his wife, gets caught up in the melee.

Anouar has his spike out, going after one of the thugs working on Said. The massive Said tears free and starts to beat the crap out of the two thugs holding him.

Max whirls away from one fight to deal with whoever is behind him. But it's Poomina, her hands holding her face together. Slowly, she takes her hands away, and blood pours through her fingers. Max sweeps her up in his arms, heads for the clinic.

MAX
Oh little girl, little girl.

This and facing page: *The riot at the clinic.*

Ashoka and his thugs observe the melee until Joan (below) gives in to the Godfather's demand.

One of the thugs throws a firebomb that hits Anouar and catches his clothing on fire. Hasari, kneeling beside Kamla, sees the match ignite the tiny leper. Without thinking, Hasari hurls himself on top of Anouar, rolling him in the dirt and against his own body to put out the flames.

An explosion in the doorway scatters anyone who remains in the area. Ashoka prowls the balcony of the clinic, ready to complete its destruction. Suddenly Joan gives up, desperate to protect what is left. She strides forward through a sea of flailing sticks, escorted by Hasari trying to shelter her, and shouts up at Ashoka.

JOAN
We'll pay! All right? We'll pay! So by all means protect us!

Ashoka raises a hand, the Goonda blows a whistle, and the fighting stops as suddenly as it began. The combatants are breathing heavily. There is silence but for the groans and cries of the wounded and grieving. Ashoka addresses the crowd.

ASHOKA
You see, these foreigners are no use to you. Turn your backs on them!

Ashoka points a finger at Hasari.

ASHOKA
Rickshaw *wallah!* I warned you about the company you keep.

Later, in the examining room. Max carefully sutures
Poomina's awful facial wound as Kamla assists him.

Max stitches Poomina's face.

KAMLA
Will she . . . her face, will it . . .

MAX
She's going to be absolutely beautiful. If you do exactly
what I tell you, there won't be any scars, sweetheart.
But you gotta stay here, understand?
(to Joan)
You have to make her stay here.

JOAN
I'll try.

MAX
Don't goddamn try, you do it!

Poomina peers through her pain at Max, his hands
putting her back together. Hasari stands in the
doorway.

MAX
(a litany)
I hate this place, I hate this place, I hate this place.

Hasari stares at Max, disappointment and accusation in
his eyes.

Ashoka crosses Hasari's name off the roster of rickshaw pullers.

[The Godfather's courtyard]
Ashoka sits behind a little table, sharpening his pencil slowly with a razor. Hasari crouches in front of him. The Goonda slouches near the table, smoking a cigarette and reading a newspaper. Other thugs watch.

ASHOKA
What have you got to say?

HASARI
I told them that your father provides us with a great deal and that I promised to be loyal to him . . .

ASHOKA
You are off the list. You will leave your rickshaw here.

HASARI
Please, Babu.

ASHOKA
Your rickshaw will be reserved for people who deserve our trust.

HASARI
Please, Babu, I'll be ruined! This is as if the ground has opened up. I must speak to Mr. Ghatak!

Hasari, frantic, starts for the house. A thug forces him to his knees, his arm twisted painfully behind his back, then slams his head on the desk. Ashoka leans across to Hasari, grabs his nose, a blade held a few inches away.

ASHOKA
My father's ill! I'm making all the decisions.

HASARI
I have a family!

ASHOKA
The decision is final. Go. Do you want him to break your fingers?

HASARI
Babu, please, let me explain.

The thug drags him off and out the gate. The Goonda padlocks it. Hasari runs to the window. The shutter is pulled down in his face. He turns and wanders off, defeated, cut off, terrified.

[Joan's room at the clinic]
Flickering candlelight illuminates the reproduction of *The Raft of the Medusa* hanging on the wall. Max rails at Joan.

MAX
I quit. I should've stayed quit! I became a doctor because my father was a goddamn doctor. I played football because he played football. I ran for class president because my daddy was class president, and I am done with it.

JOAN
Listen to me, Max. If you want to leave, tell us to stuff ourselves, but don't try and blame anyone except yourself.

MAX
All right, I quit.   Look, I have given you light years more than I ever planned. I am not Magic Max, and I don't want to be invested in these people, with their needs and their clinging and their desperation. It's just too goddamn painful!

JOAN
That's what it is, working with people, painful. And it's a struggle, not to lose compassion or humanity. But it's a struggle we can't afford to lose.

MAX
Bullshit. Ghatak is right. People are just out for themselves and everything else is a fraud. So what are you, Saint Joan? A fool or a fraud?

JOAN
Both. Both of those things. But I am here because I want to be here. Maybe the world was meant to break

"Even the simple act of throwing a few coins onto a beggar's mat raises a complex set of questions. This human knot isn't a solo act, he is a link in an economic chain. He probably pays some kind of 'rent' for the privilege of using his little patch. He certainly pays the local mafia a percentage of what he earns. The parents who sold, or gave, him into his painful bondage as a child were making a surer investment in his economic security than trying to put him through school. Give him a few coins and you contribute to the financial strength of the mafia, who in turn invest in the purchase of another human being. And yet, this is a human being lying here on his mat. He has to eat. . . . Many Indians are tender about what they see as the Westerner's obsession with their poverty. But to ignore its brutal economic cycle is to ignore a pressure that haunts all Indians whatever their social status."

Roland Joffé

Pauline Collins as "Sister Joan" Bethel

One of Britain's best-loved actresses, Pauline Collins makes her third film appearance as Joan Bethel, the strong-minded Irishwoman who runs the City of Joy Self-Help School and Dispensary to bring aid to the residents of Anand Nagar.

Known to British television and stage audiences for many years, and to American audiences through her role as Sarah in the long-running Masterpiece Theatre hit *Upstairs, Downstairs,* Collins has made her mark in films more recently. She won the British Academy Award and an Oscar nomination for her starring role in *Shirley Valentine,* having previously won the Tony, Drama Desk, and Olivier awards for her stage portrayal of the same role on Broadway and the West End.

Her numerous stage credits include London productions of *Romantic Comedy* with Tom Conti, Alan Ayckbourne's *Woman in Mind, The Importance of Being Earnest,* and Chekhov's *The Bear.*

Her reading of the *City of Joy* script made Collins eager to come to Calcutta. "First of all I wanted to play the rickshaw puller," she claims. "Of course I couldn't play Hasari, but I'm very very happy with the character of Joan." Collins's enthusiasm for the part led her to do some firsthand research in the street clinics of Calcutta, to meet the kind of people who devoted themselves to working in such places and witness the situations they encountered every day.

She also appreciated the chance to work with Roland Joffé. "What I like best is the way he takes a story with a global view and makes it very particular.

He takes a large canvas and highlights a small piece of it, so you can identify with the characters. That certainly happens in this film."

---

your heart, Max. From the moment we're born, we're shipwrecked, struggling between hope and despair, all of us.

Max begins laughing quietly, despairingly.

JOAN
God, Junior.
(*sits on the bed beside him*)
Not everyone's cut out for this, you know. You did the best you could. Better than most.

MAX
No. No I did not, lady. I messed up. I messed up bad.

JOAN
You're only a human being.

MAX
(*laughs again*)
Let us not ever forget. Run, spectate, commit.
(*points to himself*)
Running spectator.

Max is about to go out the door. Joan stops him.

JOAN

But you can't leave your demons behind. The more you run, the harder they chase you.

Max slams the door behind him. As he lunges into the square, he meets Kamla's eyes and looks away.

Hasari, drunk, comes down the slope and face to face with Max.

HASARI

They took away my rickshaw.

Kamla's hand flies to her mouth. Hasari peers at Max with drunken eyes. It's an awful moment for Max.

MAX

So what do you want me to do about it, get it back for you?

He takes a step away and stops.

MAX

Look, I'm sorry. I'm going home, okay?

Hasari stares at Max. On the roof, the children listen. At the tea shop, the late-night talkers listen.

"If you are a good man, then on a tamarind leaf you can accommodate nine."

Bengali saying

HASARI
But we trusted you.

MAX
Well, that was your goddamn mistake—all of you!

Max walks away. Disbelief follows him. Kamla moves to Hasari's side.

HASARI
You will not have anything to do with the clinic or those people anymore!

Ram joins them.

RAM
What I earn is yours, too.

Hasari touches his friend and goes into the hut. Alone in his pain, he spots his tea caddy in which he planted his seeds over a month ago. He bends over to tenderly touch the growing shoot. He looks up, and the three children are staring at him. What will their father do now to keep them alive?

AMRITA
We have what you've saved for my dowry, Father.

An unbearable thought. Hasari waters the growing shoot.

PART III

✦ EVERYTHING NOT GIVEN IS LOST ✦

❖ Everything Not Given Is Lost ❖

Hasari at the blood bank.

[A street blood bank]
A needle is injected into Hasari's arm, and blood flows into a bottle. Seated on a stool, Hasari watches his blood leave his body, his face broken out in perspiration. His is face immobile, his thoughts distant. The attendant starts to pull the needle out, but Hasari stops his hand.

HASARI
Take some more.

The attendant shrugs and walks off, as the blood continues to flow.

Back outside, barely ambulatory, Hasari starts down the street, but has to stop and lean against a wall. He has a ferocious coughing fit.

When Hasari returns home to the City of Joy, he pauses in the door as he finds Max sitting with Kamla and Amrita. The two men stare at each other. Amrita goes out. Hasari ignores Max and goes up the stairs. Max tries to get through to him.

MAX
Hasari, I know you feel I let you down, but don't punish Kamla. What happened was between you and me, and we need her at the clinic.

Hasari continues on upstairs. Kamla joins Max, who tries once more.

MAX
Hasari, please.

After a moment of silence, Kamla exchanges looks with Max and follows Hasari up the stairs. He is curled up on the bed. She sits down.

KAMLA
The clinic is for everyone, and I think they will pay me.

Hasari bolts up, anger and jealousy on his face we've never seen.

HASARI
No more clinic. I'm your husband and you'll do what I say! Stay away from him. He is not one of us. This is

Hasari was guided to the blood bank by a man who "belonged to a profession practiced in abundance in a city where the slightest suggestion of profit inevitably attracted a swarm of parasitical intermediaries known as 'middlemen.' . . . [This one] tracked down donors for one of the numerous private blood banks that flourished in Calcutta. His technique was always the same. He went prowling around the entrances to the work sites, factories, markets, anywhere he knew he would find men without work, ready to agree to anything for the sake of a few rupees. The taboos of Islam forbad Muslims to sell their blood. He was, therefore, interested only in Hindus.

"For a man at the end of his resources, the sale of his blood represented a last chance of survival, and for astute and unscrupulous businessmen this meant the opportunity to make a fortune."

Dominique Lapierre,
The City of Joy

Oh, what a heavy bag!
No, it is an elephant;
He is an awful weight,
Let us throw his palkee down,
Let us see him in the mud—
Let us leave him to his fate.
Ay, but he will beat us then
With a thick stick.
Then let's make haste and get along
Jump along quickly.

Street song of a palkee-bearer carrying a clergyman, transcribed by Lola Montez, 1841

not his home and he is a tree with no roots.

Kamla tries to interrupt.

HASARI
He will only be good to you as long as you please him.

MAX
That's just not true, Hasari.

HASARI
Please don't teach me what is true! Just leave us alone.

Max goes outside.

HASARI
(turns to Kamla)
I have lost my rickshaw. I have lost my livelihood.

[Leper colony]
Max walks through the village with Anouar, who is carried by Said.

ANOUAR
Max, I have something confidential to ask you. This disease of ours is not a visitation for past sins, but an illness, correct?

MAX
Right.

ANOUAR
I want to start a workshop. We have weavers and carpenters. We could weave cloth instead of begging.

MAX
It's a good idea, but . . .

ANOUAR
Listen, Max. I know this Godfather. He is a clever man. He's got everyone to turn their backs on you, but I know a way you can work your way back into their hearts. That's why I want to show you something. Come with me.

He leads Max into a small yard, where the two pullers, Chomotkar and Ramatullah, pull back a tarp to reveal a battered rickshaw, the springs poking out of the seat, the broken wheels lying in the body, the finish scarred and gouged, one shaft broken. Anouar and Said look on proudly.

MAX
You devils. You steal this?

RAMATULLAH
The police, Sahib, they stole it. We borrowed it from them.

Om Puri as Hasari Pal

One of India's most distinguished actors and a veteran of some 100 films, Om Puri takes the pivotal role of Hasari Pal, the dispossessed peasant who finds both despair and hope in the streets of Calcutta, and a complex relationship with the foreigner Max Lowe.

Puri's career is based in India's art cinema, and his films often carry a social message. Born in the Punjab, in northern India, he graduated from the National School of Drama in Delhi and studied film acting at the Film Institute in Pune. His many roles include *Sadgati,* directed by India's great film auteur Satyajit Ray, *Arohan,* for which Puri won India's National Award, and *Ardh Satya,* which earned him Czechoslovakia's Karlovy Vary Award. He has been seen by Western audiences in *Gandhi* and *Jewel in the Crown.* In 1990 Puri was honored with the Indian government's prestigious Padmasri Award, given to leaders in various fields for their contribution to society and their profession.

His performance as Hasari in *City of Joy* is profoundly convincing. He practiced at length with a rickshaw in the streets of Calcutta, an experience he describes on page 57. Roland Joffé notes that "one reason I chose Om is because he has a village background. He knows that background; it is in his hands, and in the way his body moves."

[Interior of a storage shed, City of Joy]
Slatted, shafted light penetrates the dark space. Hasari watches Max flip the tarpaulin off the broken rickshaw.

MAX
I know it's a little ratty. I'm good with my hands. You're good with yours. That can be fixed. What do you think?

Hasari looks at the rickshaw, can't resist touching it, examining the hood, then drops it. Max is part resentful, part touched.

HASARI
If I were to go on the streets with this machine, I would die in a gutter with my throat cut.

MAX
Nope. I got it all figured out. The license, the cops, all that can be fixed with bribes or something. As for the Godfather, we just don't work in his area. We'll have nothing to do with the sucker.

Max picks up the wheel of the rickshaw, passes it over to Hasari.

MAX
Please, take it.

Hasari takes the wheel. After a moment, he lays it down.

MAX
Damn it, Hasari!

HASARI
Dr. Max, you don't understand.

MAX
Tell me.

HASARI
You're a *gora*. A white man. You're different. You think you can buy people's hearts by giving them things, building clinics, playing a big man. For me, trust is in the heart. That is something that cannot be purchased.

MAX
Purchased. Is that what you think? Is that what you really feel? Okay, fine, all right.

Max flings the tarpaulin back over the rickshaw as Hasari speaks.

HASARI
I am a small man. I was born small. That's my fate, and I will not allow you to tempt me again with big thoughts.

Max, now furious, moves very close to Hasari.

MAX
Oh no, no sir. Small isn't the word for you, pal! You're a little brown, illiterate, gutless victim and you should take all this crap from the cops and the gangsters! And you should keep locking your wife up, being suspicious, being jealous for no goddamn reason!

HASARI
You have no right to speak such things to me!

Max shoves Hasari again, trying to incite him.

MAX
Then stop me! I didn't do all this on my own, Hasari. You participated too! Did I take your goddamn rickshaw? Did I make you live in this shithole? You want to be pissed at me, fine, but why don't you get pissed at the people who are really using you?!
(turns to go, then turns back)
But you know what I think? I think you should bow down so low you don't have to get up.

Max storms out, leaving Hasari on his own.

[Clinic, City of Joy]

Max is working carefully on Poomina, taking the compresses off her healing scars, when something outside the window catches his attention. Shambu, carrying teacups, looks this way and that, and then sneaks into the storage shed.

We hear a tap, tap, tap. The door is half open, the padlock hanging on its chain. Max opens the door. Hasari is working on the rickshaw, with Manooj helping and Shambu sewing the seat.

MAX
Aha! Busted!
(comes closer)
Rickshaw *wallahs* eat your heart out. It's already looking great.

HASARI
Shambu, close the door. The Godfather has more eyes than a pineapple. Manooj, bring that stand.

Max attempts to help Hasari. Hasari drops the rickshaw.

HASARI
Please, let me do it!

Manooj wedges a bench underneath the rickshaw.

"The relationship between Max and Hasari reflects in a sense the historical relationship between the English and India. Max does teach Hasari to stand up for himself and value himself, and the British did bring democracy to India. But then the Indians said: Look, wait a minute, if we are fond of you and if you believe in these things and want us to adopt them, then you must leave us alone and let us put them into practice ourselves. I think all that is hinted at in the relationship of Max and Hasari."

Roland Joffé

Repairs begin on the rickshaw and the friendship.

Posters advertising the products of India's thriving film industry are a vivid part of the street scene in every large city. Photo by Robert Holmes.

HASARI
Push it under the rod.

MAX
Hasari, I promised the kids I'd take them to the cinema to the new Anil Kapur movie.

Shambu and Manooj look back hopefully.

HASARI
If a man promises something, he must do it.

Hasari picks up one of the wheels, turns his back on Max. Then he explodes in a coughing fit. He tries to control it. Can't. Has to spit something into his hand. Max takes his hand.

MAX
Can I see that please?

Hasari tries to pull his hand away.

HASARI
It's nothing, it's a cough.

MAX
If it's nothing, open your hand.

He pries Hasari's fingers open. There is bloody phlegm in the palm.

MAX
You're not taking the medication, are you? Hasari, not everything I do is wrong. I'm a doctor. Tuberculosis is not something to be messed with. It can kill you. But you know best.

Max goes out. Hasari stares after him.

Outside the movie theater, Max and the kids engage in a mock sword fight as they start to walk home. They don't at first notice the bright beams of a truck coming at them, but then it gains speed and is clearly trying to run them down. Max manages to push them all out of the street just in time.

[Self-help workshop, City of Joy]
Men are loading boxes and discussing the incident of the night before.

ASHISH
Look, the Godfather is against everybody. He's trying to put his thumb on all of us.

DR. SUNIL
No, I don't think is was an accident. I don't think it was the little boys; I think it was Max they were aiming at.

ASHISH
Max is not the point. He is doing this to frighten all of us. Max has nothing to do with this—in fact, the Godfather has nothing to do with this. It's his son. Don't tell me that before Max came nothing like this ever happened.

[Storage shed]
Ram, Chomoktar, and Hasari are working on the old rickshaw.

CHOMOKTAR
Isn't it a work of art?

RAM
This is Arjuna's chariot.

CHOMOKTAR
Pity it won't be used.

HASARI
Why?

Hasari puts the final touches on the new rickshaw.
Overleaf: *Rickshaws assembled in preparation for shooting the strike scene.*

Arjuna is the heroic warrior-prince of the Hindu gospel *Bhagavad-Gita* (Song of God). Preparing for a great battle, Arjuna calls upon the god incarnate Krishna to be his personal counselor and charioteer, and the two figures are often depicted in Hindu art in Arjuna's chariot. The image of a chariot at war speaks strongly to the human horses of Calcutta.

Near the start of the epic, Arjuna says:

> Krishna the changeless
> Halt my chariot
> There where the warriors,
> Bold for the battle,
> Face their foemen.
> Between the armies
> There let me see them . . .

Bhagavad-Gita

Ashoka threatens the striking pullers.

CHOMOKTAR
Will they let you?

HASARI
I am going to speak to the old man. I'll wait and catch him when he is alone.

CHOMOKTAR
Listen to him!

HASARI
He's not like the son. He came to the city with a little bundle.

Hasari goes towards the door.

CHOMOKTAR
Hasari, don't . . .

HASARI
They could have killed my little son yesterday.

CHOMOKTAR
It could be you tomorrow and then what will happen to your family?

Hasari goes out the door.

[The Zamindar's house]
Hasari passes an ambulance on his way to the Godfather's house, and arrives to an outcry of anger. There are several dozen rickshaws and more arriving by the minute.

HASARI
What's going on?

CHOMOKTAR
The Godfather is dying! The son is raising the rent!

Ashoka is on his front steps with a loudspeaker before a growing crowd of pullers. He's backed up by the Goonda and a dozen of his thugs. The loudspeaker lifts Ashoka's voice above the anger.

ASHOKA
Do you know how much it costs to change the spoke in a wheel? Or how much *baksheesh* I have to pay the police?

Impulsively, Hasari moves forward, his eyes on Ashoka. Cries from pullers: "Who will be the victims of this madness? You?" "Hell no!" "You don't need the six rupees each old crate brings you per day to fill your belly! For us, it means death!"

The street is so packed with rickshaws and pullers now that cars can't get through. A chorus of horns honk; Hasari stands at the front beside his friends Ramtullah and Chomotkar, who scream with the others.

Rassoul steps up on a *telagarhi* with a loudspeaker.

Above: *Hasari exhorts the strikers.*
Below: *Ashoka's thugs silence Hasari.*

Zindabad! The Rickshaw Revolt

When the rickshaw pullers in *City of Joy* go on strike over an attempted increase in the daily rent they pay on their vehicles, they are carrying on a struggle for fair treatment that goes back many years. It began in 1948, when the owners had demanded that every vehicle should bring in two sets of fees, one for daytime and the other for nighttime use.

"This claim had been the cause of their first strike, an eighteen-day *hartal* [work stoppage] which had ended with victory for the human horses and the formation of a union." Its founder, a former Bihari peasant named Golam Rassoul, "had realized that a powerful union was the only means by which the population of rickshaw *wallahs* could make its voice heard. Unlike the factory workers, however, the pullers worked individually and their limited ambitions made it extremely difficult to get them together for collective action."

At first few were attracted to meetings of the Rickshaw Work-

Rickshaw pullers with the banner of their union. Photo by Dominique Lapierre.

ers Union, but over thirty years "Rassoul had fought relentlessly. With protest meetings, hunger marches, and strikes, he had inspired and organized the resistance of the human horses of Calcutta against the voracity of their employers and the interference of the police."

The signal used by the pullers to gather their forces was to strike the bells they carried against the rickshaw shafts. "'Some men have knives to defend themselves, or guns, or even worse weapons,' says Hasari Pal. 'All we had was a little ball of copper about the size of a betel nut. But that poor little bell . . . was mightier than any weapon. It was the voice of the rickshaws of Calcutta—our voice.'"

Dominique Lapierre,
The City of Joy

RASSOUL

Listen to me! Listen now!
(when the pullers quiet)
Friends! I ask you to vote for an unlimited strike. *Inkalabad zindabad!* Long live the revolution! Rickshaw Workers Union *zindabad!*

A strike? No income at all? The slogan is taken up by a small percentage of the assemblage. Fear and doubt on most faces.

ASHOKA

Those of you who want to strike, leave your rickshaws here! Those who want to work—customers are waiting! Get out!

Most of the pullers begin to back away, to yield.
But something detonates in Hasari, and he jumps onto the *telagarhi* and grabs the microphone from

Ashoka. Police arrive in vans.

HASARI
Brothers! Don't go! Don't go . . .

A signal from Ashoka and one of the thugs knocks Hasari down. A number of the pullers come forward and a riot starts. The police move in, beat and arrest many of the demonstrators—including Hasari.

[Bonsal Court]
The room has a barred cage running around its edge; the cage is filled to overflowing. Hasari stands before the judge, his face covered with blood, his body a mass of aches and welts. At the back of the room, Max and Kamla; elsewhere, Ashoka, the Goonda, and several of his thugs.

HASARI
I am proud to carry my countrymen from place to place, and I thank the gods for work. But the life of a rickshaw puller is hard. The boiling asphalt blisters our feet, our noses burn from the fumes of motor cars and buses, our backs curve from the loads we pull. We are threatened by corrupt police. We pay off officials and goondas. But sometimes it just builds up and builds up, and you can't take it anymore. I will not keep silent anymore, and I will not be cheated and threatened. Life is hard enough. No more.

Hasari stands up in court: "I will not be silent anymore."

The Bonsal Court, Calcutta's municipal court, "was an old brick building on the other side of Dalhousie Square, in the center of town. . . . [Near the entrance] a crowd was squeezed in between a double row of vendors. The warm air intensified the smell of hot oil and frying. Farther away . . . people were lining up for the public writers, who squatted behind typewriters. Inside the courtyard, others were having coconuts cut open or drinking tea or bottled drinks. There were even beggars on the steps up to the audience chambers. What was most striking, however, was the constant coming and going."

Dominique Lapierre,
The City of Joy

The City of Joy celebrates the monsoon's arrival.

Ramatullah starts to applaud. Rassoul follows suit. The judge bangs her gavel.

JUDGE
Silence!
(when it's silent)
There will be no commotion. I will make a restraining order against Ashoka Ghatak. This man *(indicating Hasari)* will be permitted to use his rickshaw without let or hindrance. These workers have a clear and legal right to strike.

Cheers from the pullers. Several corrupt police look at each other, at Ashoka. The judge bangs her gavel again.

JUDGE
I haven't finished these proceedings. For his part in this disturbance, I fine the defendant fifty rupees.

HASARI
Fifty rupees, Your Honor?

JUDGE
Pay at this time or spend seven days in jail!

Seven days in jail will cost him far more than fifty rupees. As he reaches for his screw of money, a hand suddenly protrudes into the cage through the bars.

RAMATULLAH
Hasari!

And now another hand with several rupees reaches through.

RASSOUL
Hasari!

Now a dozen voices call his name and a dozen hands reach through the bars with rupees clutched in their fists and press the money into Hasari's hands. The judge, Max and Kamla, and certainly Ashoka watch this in amazement.

    Max turns, shoots a little finger gun and winks at Ashoka. Close on Ashoka; on his face, we see pure hatred for these two men.

At last one day the storm clouds gather overhead and the long-delayed monsoon rains arrive. Children and adults dance in the square, turned instantly into a muddy swamp. Men tear off their shirts, women rush out fully clothed, singing. Swarms of naked children run about.

    Ashoka still nurses his grudge against Max. One night he and several of his thugs sneak into Max's room at the Green Acres Hotel and render Max helpless with a wet towel wrapped around his head as he sleeps. Once again, he is beaten and threatened with death if he does not leave Calcutta.

[The square, City of Joy]
Max runs through the rain, carrying his belongings, and pounds on the gate of the clinic. Joan opens the door in her Indian pajamas. One look at him is enough.

JOAN
What's happened?

MAX
Ashoka ordered me to go home. So here I am.

No words can describe the *chataka*,
the rain-bird's love
for the cloud
and its water.
Clouds deceive it so
and yet, flies the bird,
eager to seize,
gazing, gazing at the clouds,
never blinking.

The way of all *chatakas*
is the death of thirst.
They will not drink
unless clouds break. . . .

    The Baul poet Lalan, from
    Songs of the Bards of Bengal

*Bristi parey tapur tupur nadi elo
    ban
Shibu Thakur biyey holo tin kanya
    dan
Ek banyaradhen baren ek kanya
    khan
Ek kanyarag korey baper bari jan*

*(Pitter patter falls the rain—tidal
    bore over the river.
Shibu Thakur gets married—three
    daughters given away.
One daughter cooks, and one
    daughter eats,
One daughter in anger goes over
    to her father's place.)*

Bengali nonsense rhyme

[An upstairs room at the clinic]
By candlelight, Max unpacks his things, Joan helping him stow them. He takes a photograph of himself and a young girl, sticks it up on the wall. Joan glances at it.

JOAN
Who's that? Who's the little girl?

MAX
A patient. She died. I couldn't save her. The proverbial last straw.

JOAN
There was a man in the town when I grew up. Thirteen years his wife had been dead. He still set a place for her at the table. One day he burnt the house to the ground. We never saw him again. We assumed he was a free man. Goodnight, sleep well.

He reaches for her. Kisses her cheek.

JOAN
Welcome home, Junior.

The rains seem to bring everyone to life. Hasari comes out of the house one day to go off to work, and sees the young man Subash standing in the pouring rain, waiting for Amrita. He knows what's

on the young man's mind. They exchange a few words, and he promises to visit Subash's father, who owns the metal shop where Hasari's children work.

[*Subash's house*]
Kamla and three women huddle beside a window, Amrita half hidden behind them. We pan across a staircase to another window, through which we see a doorway. In the doorway, Subash turns to smile a shy smile at Amrita; he shrugs. Past him now we see Hasari facing Subash's father and three uncles, surly men with hair matted with mustard oil.

Mr. Ghosh and the uncles stare at Hasari, who sits politely and hopefully before them.

MR. GHOSH
You're a rickshaw puller, am I correct?

HASARI
Yes, that's correct.

He looks at his brothers. They look at him.

MR. GHOSH
And I a partner in the workshop where your daughter is employed. Were you aware of that?

HASARI
Yes, yes, I was, my daughter told me, thank you.

MR. GHOSH
Yes, well then perhaps you can tell me why I would permit my son to marry your daughter.

Mr. Ghosh raises his palms. It's all over as far as he's concerned.

UNCLE 1
Just a moment, please.

The brothers huddle, whisper just loudly enough for Hasari to hear.

UNCLE 1
Are you saying there's no way you'd consider this match?

Mr. Ghosh shakes his head, shrugs his palms.

UNCLE 1
Perhaps some inducement? Would that be of any help?

MR. GHOSH
(*considering this*)
What could he possibly offer?

UNCLE 1
Probably nothing. But perhaps, in fairness, we should find out.

"Amrita, the rickshaw puller's daughter, was only thirteen years old but if the cruel years on the pavement and in the shantytown had not tarnished her freshness, the gravity of her expression bespoke the fact that she had long since ceased to be a child. The role of a girl in Indian society is a thankless one. No domestic task, no drudgery is considered too much for her. . . . A mother before ever having children of her own, Amrita had brought up her brothers. It was she who had guided their first steps, foraged for their food in the hotel refuse, sewn together rags that served as their clothes. . . . Right from her earliest years, her mother had unflaggingly prepared her for the one big event of her life, the one which for a day would transform a child of poverty into the subject of all the conversation in the small world of the poor who surrounded her: her marriage."

Dominique Lapierre,
The City of Joy

The giant crane sprays water on Om Puri and the crew during one of the monsoon scenes.

Making a Monsoon

The monsoon embracing India in two life-saving, watery arms each year is the country's lifeline, revitalizing an earth parched by the relentless sun.

"To the former peasant, banished forever from his land by drought," writes Dominique Lapierre, "every year that first drop of water was like 'manna from the heavens and proof that the gods could still weep for the plight of mankind on this earth.'" Should the monsoon fail, the inevitable result is drought and famine—phenomena all too common in Hasari Pal's home province of Bihar. If it is late, prayers and songs are offered up, and rainmakers brought in to appease the gods.

The makers of *City of Joy*

turned to more reliable means to produce the monsoon that floods Calcutta midway through the film. Special Effects Director Nick Allder (*Alien*, the *Star Wars* trilogy, *Jewel of the Nile*) assembled a vast plumbing system that dumped 250,000 gallons of water an hour on the set and sprayed torrential rain on actual city streets. Because Calcutta has no fire hydrants, an 850-foot well was sunk 15 miles away, supplying water to holding tanks with a total capacity of 750,000 gallons. The entire bustee set (measuring 500 by 200 feet) was built inside a giant concrete tank to contain the flood.

Several thousand feet of steel piping with rain jets were plumbed into the set buildings, and a 30-ton crane modified to

inject rain into any part of the set from 100 feet up. The crane alone could pump 500 gallons of water a minute, and four wind machines created winds up to 70 mph. The water used to make rain in the streets was transported from the well by giant tanks mounted on flatbed trucks. As standing pipes and the crane showered monsoon rain onto the heads of stars, extras, and slow-moving passersby, one local commented, "It was a mind-boggling and magnificent sight."

Allder has created many rain and storm sequences in his thirty year career in special effects, "but nothing to compare with this film," he says. "I have never made rain over such a large area."

Hasari redoubles his efforts to swell Amrita's dowry. He is determined that the match will be made. The monsoon has arrived just in time to help his cause. At times, rickshaws are the only vehicles that can pass through the flooded streets, so a puller can make good money by working hard during the rains.

Hasari and his fellow pullers welcome the monsoon.

[The rickshaw station]
The rain pours down. People clamor for rickshaws. The line moves forward as fast as the pullers can take on passengers. Hasari, Ram, Ramatullah, Chomotkar looks at the stalled buses, the streetcars, the taxis, the private cars.

CHOMOTKAR
What a joy it is to survey this disaster! We'll make a fortune!

HASARI
The monsoon is the great Durga's gift to the human horse!

Hasari glances at Ram, who isn't a part of the joking.

HASARI
What's the matter?

RAM
I'm wet and I'm cold. Your daughter is getting married. Time is passing. I want to go home to my wife.

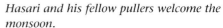

Max gets ready to throw Anouar to the rescuers.
Photo by Stephen F. Morley.

[Wedding shop]
Water pours down. From here, we see Hasari inside, putting money down in front of the shop owner and then hustling back into the rain and taking up his shafts. We watch the owner look after him with a touch of disdain as he comes into the window and takes down the beautiful green and gold sari.

[The mud bank on the road to the leper colony]
The big mute Said runs, followed by Hasari and a phalanx of rickshaw pullers: Chomotkar, Rassoul, Rama-tullah. Also Joan, Kamla, Manooj, several others in the rickshaws, Max and Sunil, each with his doctor bag—all of them running in silhouette along the embankment in the rain.

ARISTOTLE JOHN
Where can we take them? We can't take them back to the clinic. No one will put up with it.

CHOMOTKAR
We can't let them down, can we? Eh, Max Daddah?

As they reach the little colony, a flash of lightning illuminates the scene. Water up to the roof of the little structures. The more able-bodied are trying to ferry the sick or infirm to the highest structures. Meeta and her baby are on a roof. The mudbank is too slippery for them to clamber up.

The rescuers start throwing rubber tires and ropes into the floodwaters to aid the swimmers. Hasari wades over to Meeta in neck-high water and takes her baby; others help her off the roof to safety.

Anouar is trapped on the roof of the most distant structure, and Max swims over to him. He picks the little man up and is about to swim him to shore, when a large tree above them suddenly topples, its roots loosened by the swirling waters. Max looks upwards at a shout from one of the rickshaw pullers, and with a desperate heave, literally throws Anouar towards the outstretched hands waiting for him.

Barely has he done so when the tree strikes his head, knocking him into the water. Before the horrified eyes of the watchers, he goes under.

Immediately, Hasari dives into the maelstrom, risks his own life to save Max. Max has disappeared. And now Hasari, too, disappears. After some moments, Hasari surfaces, spewing filth out of his mouth. He dives again, comes up somewhere else. Dives a third time. Then he bursts out of the filth, dragging the unconscious Max towards safety.

[Max's room, the clinic]
Max lies in bed, all of the Pals anxiously watching for him to regain consciousness, along with Said holding Anouar. Others are nearby, watching.

Shambu calls to him.

SHAMBU
Max Daddah! Max Daddah!

Max opens his eyes, looks around the room. Holds his hand out to Hasari, who moves to him.

MAX
You people. I really love you guys.

HASARI
All that is given is not lost, Max Daddah. You are cold. Joan Di . . .

Hasari gestures to the others to leave. They go out the door as Joan comes in with tea.

MAX
. . . in bed when he should be working . . .

JOAN
Ssssh, there now, lie back.
(eases him back down)
I am glad you stuck it out.

Durga on her lion killing Mahishasura, c. 1855-1860. From Kalighat Paintings.

"She is the triumphant goddess, the destructor of the demons of evil and ignorance, wife of the god Shiva, daughter of the Himalayas, a queen of manifold incarnations, the feminine force of the gods, alternately the symbol of gentleness and of cruelty. The Puranas, the golden legends of Hinduism, devote thousands of verses to the legendary exploits she accomplishes under a score of names, guises, and attributes.

"In her tender guise she is called Ouma, light and grace; Gauri, the goddess with the light skin; Parvati, queen of the mountains; or Jagan Mata, mother of the universe. In her destructive form she takes the names of Kali the Black one, Bhairavi the Terrible, Chandi the Furious, or Durga the unattainable. It is under this latter name and in the guise of the divine conqueror of evil that she is specially worshipped in Bengal."

Dominique Lapierre,
The City of Joy

My life is a little oil lamp
Floating on the waves.
But from which landing-pier
Did you set me afloat?
With darkness ahead of me
and darkness behind,
Darkness overlaps my night—
While the necklace of waves
Constantly rings.
The storm of the night
Relentlessly flows
Below the stars,
And the lamp is afloat
On the shoreless space—
As my company. . . .

The Baul poet Gangaram,
from *Songs of the Bards of Bengal*

MAX
People grow older; sometimes they even grow up.

Joan hands him the tea.

JOAN
Drink this, it will warm you up. Sorry, it's a bit full.

Max puts down the tea and lies back.

MAX
You know that time at the Godfather's, when you wanted to know about the candy and the bribes?

When I was a kid, I walked in on my father with another woman. That's when the bribes started. He'd tell my Mom we were going to play golf. I loved driving that golf cart for him. I loved being with him. Then we stopped going to the golf course. We'd go to see her instead.

He kept a stock of candy bars in the glove compartment. "Don't tell Mom. This is just between us men. Okay?" I'd sit at the dinner table, and I couldn't even look at my mother. After a while, I couldn't even eat the candy bars. I just stuck 'em in a drawer. So at nine, I was an alibi and a traitor. When I was twelve, she died, and I never told her. After that, I just shut down.

JOAN
Shut the world out maybe.

MAX
I worshipped the ground he walked upon.

JOAN
Lonely, lonely Max.

MAX
Lonely Joan.

JOAN
Sometimes.

MAX
You know what this is?
(cranking his thumb in a circular motion)
The world's smallest record player playing "My heart bleeds for you."

They both laugh. Max turns away.

MAX
Oh God, I'm so cold.

After a moment, Joan stands up, slips out of her shirt, slips under the blanket, her skin against his.

MAX
Oh God, you're so warm.

They hold each other, these two friends.

PART IV

✤ THE LIGHT OF THE WORLD ✤

❖ THE LIGHT OF THE WORLD ❖

[Ram's house, City of Joy]
A group is gathered on a dry, sunny afternoon, peering into the hut. We focus on the growing flower in the tea caddy in the window and then go through the window into the Pals' room.

Hasari, the local *hara giri*, or marriage broker, Mr. Ghosh, and the Ghosh uncles are crammed into the tiny room. Members of our group jam the doorway, spectating. We can only hear a babble of arguing from out here.

Max approaches, and Shambu runs into his arms.

MAX
Ram, how's it going?

RAM
They're very upset. They say that Hasari has sent his daughter to trap the son. But all that really stands between them is a single ounce of gold.

MAX
I probably have that much in my teeth. What do you think?

Max opens his mouth for Shambu. Shambu peers in as we hear Hasari exclaim

HASARI (O.C.)
That's robbery! The child of a rajah might be worth that, and I'm not even sure of that! Impossible.

MAX
(to Shambu)
Sounds like we're very close.

Max peers over heads into the hut and Shambu presses close to him.

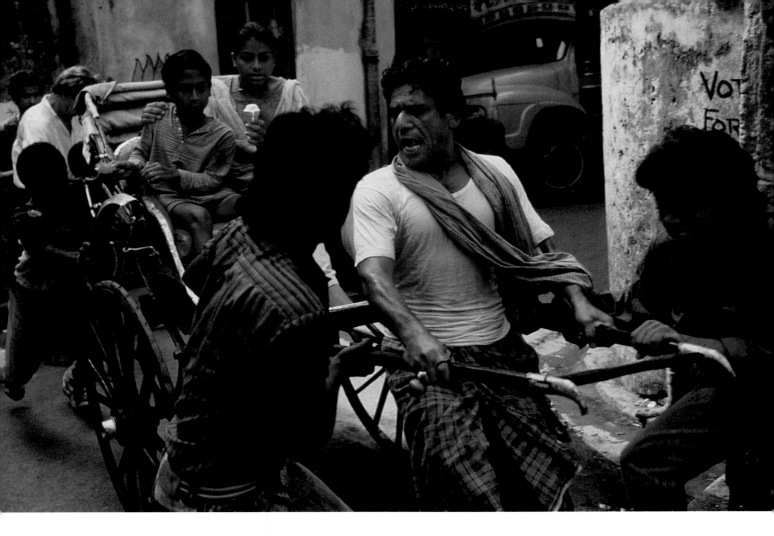

[Headmistress's office, St. Pius School]
Sister Cecelia, in full habit, looks over a sheaf of test scores. Then she peers up at Manooj, seated between Hasari and Max.

SISTER CECILIA
Well, indeed I think Sister Joan is right. We've got a prospect here. We'll start you off with a few classes; if that works out, we'll make a proper student of you.

Hasari can't believe his ears. Manooj sits frozen. Max grins.

[Narrow lane, near City of Joy]
Amrita, Subash, and Shambu are heading home from the workshop. Subash flirts with Amrita. They see Hasari, Max, and Manooj coming toward them. Manooj runs to them, shouting that he's going to the school; Amrita, Subash, Shambu congratulate him.

Subash departs and the rest continue toward home. Suddenly several of Ashoka's thugs appear from alleyways, grab the rickshaw shafts, and herd everyone into a small courtyard, as trucks swing around to block both

Ashoka's men wrestle for control of Hasari's rickshaw.

"I do whatever I like. I'm in charge."

ends of the lane. Hasari runs up to Ashoka, who sits in the courtyard. The kids huddle instinctively together in fear, clinging to Max. Retribution, it would seem, has arrived.

HASARI
What are you doing? This is my rickshaw! Babu, what is this?

ASHOKA
(putting his palms together in mock greeting)
Thank you for dropping by.
(conversationally)
My father is dead. So now I'm in charge. Is this your rickshaw? You made this?
(approaches rickshaw)
It is beautiful! Blue! Beautiful!

He gets into the seat, deliberately takes out a narrow bladed knife, and staring at Hasari, begins to slice up the newly covered seats of the rickshaw. Max looks around, trying to cool things.

MAX
Ashoka, please don't do this.

ASHOKA
I do whatever I like. I'm in charge.

Art Malik as Ashoka

The accomplished actor Art Malik is most familiar to American audiences from his role as the tragic hero Hari Kumar in *The Jewel in the Crown*, the TV adaptation of Paul Scott's chronicle of the last days of the British Raj. In *City of Joy* he is a convincing heavy, playing the Godfather's volatile and brutal son, Ashoka.

Malik's family is from Pakistan, where he was born, but moved to England when he was three. Malik was classically trained at the Guildhall School of Drama and worked his way through provincial repertory to the Old Vic and the Royal Shakespeare Company.

The role of Hari Kumar brought him recognition as well as a deeper understanding of himself and his dual heritage. "It brought me finally from being a Pakistani actor living in England," he says, "to becoming an English actor who happens to have been born in Pakistan." The dark side of the British experience on the Indian subcontinent is manifested in Ashoka's bitterness toward the foreigners who have invaded his "turf."

Malik has played major roles in David Lean's *A Passage to India*, the James Bond film *Living Daylights*, and *Turtle Beach*, with Greta Scaachi and Joan Chen, among other films. He has also worked extensively in television drama.

(to Hasari)
You will get off my streets . . .
(to Max)
You will leave my country. And the clinic and school . . . closed.

MAX
Why? We're not doing you any harm.

ASHOKA
Because I hate interfering foreigners who think they're better than me.

MAX
But you hurt your own people.

ASHOKA
Exactly—my people.
(goes to Hasari and takes him by the ear)
Loyal.

Now one of the thugs grabs Amrita and shoves her toward Ashoka. Max protests, and is halted at knifepoint by another thug. Ashoka glides toward the petrified Amrita. The Goonda remains unmoving, watchful. Ashoka puts out his hand with its rings, and strokes Amrita's cheek.

A thug holds Max at bay.

Facing page: "No more feet on our necks."

ASHOKA
She is beautiful! Beautiful! Someday she is going to give somebody a lot of joy.

HASARI
Leave my child alone.

Hasari glances over his shoulder, his eyes bouncing off the Goonda's impassive face.

ASHOKA
What did he say?

MAX
He said don't touch her.

ASHOKA
What concern is it of yours, Doctor, who I touch?

MAX
They're my family.

Hasari and Max look at each other; Hasari realizes Max will die for him and his family. And now the knife comes out of Ashoka's pocket, snaps open, glints in the light. Slowly he takes Amrita's face and puts a finger in her cheek, as he did before mutilating Poomina.

MAX
No!

He lunges toward Ashoka, but the thugs intercept him and beat him to the ground.

Now even the Goonda realizes Ashoka is out of control. Ashoka grabs Amrita roughly and stares at Hasari as he deliberately fondles her breast.

And now Hasari explodes toward Ashoka, landing a hard punch to his chest. As Ashoka stumbles and falls to one knee, he knifes Hasari in the belly.

Two of the thugs make a move to come to Ashoka's rescue, but a curious thing stops them: the Goonda's

"On a farm in Uttar Pradesh I once watched a taut, thin man work a cane-cutting machine, no more than two broken scythe blades bolted to a wheel, spun by a worn rubber belt and driven by an old diesel engine. Nearby stood his boss, a Jat farmer, a big handsome man under his Sikh turban. He is running for local office and is preoccupied with the issue of loyalty; few these days value it, he says. To illustrate his point, the farmer beckons the laborer over to show me his hands, one of them indescribably mangled by the cutting machine. 'He still works for me,' rumbles the Jat fiercely. 'That is loyalty, no?' Three years later and still no safety screen; indeed this is a loyal worker. But my first assumption is wrong: the loyalty is on the part of the farmer, who troubles to keep on such a maimed specimen.

"I wonder why the laborer doesn't rip the head off his master. I ask if he has a family. His boss thinks that he has, but 'No matter, he has no story to tell anyway.' The man goes back to his work and, after a moment, glances up at me, never breaking his rhythm. He glances at his hand, then at the shirt-stretching girth of his master's back, and gives that indefinable wiggle of the head that is the Indian way of saying the unsayable. I think I hear a voice in my head: 'Life is so. I do not know if it should be so, but so it is.'"

Roland Joffé

arm, outstretched across their path, his eyes alerting them not to proceed. Max lurches to his feet unsteadily.

ASHOKA
Bhose, help me!

Hasari unloads a punch into Ashoka's face; Ashoka's nose pours blood; he starts to whimper. He clutches Hasari and holds him. Hasari struggles, slams his palm into Ashoka's chin, sending Ashoka to the ground, sending the knife skidding across the ground. Hasari straddles Ashoka, begins to pound him and pound him, intent on killing him.

But now Hasari fixes on the face of his little son, Shambu, who peers at his father, tears running down his cheeks, releasing both his boundless love for his father as well as his fear of this violent world.

Max discovers that Hasari is seriously wounded.

"Be truthful, gentle, and fearless."

Mahatma Gandhi

SHAMBU
No, Baba! No, Baba!

Hasari can't bring his fist down again. A beat. He rises and looks down at Ashoka beneath him.

HASARI
No more. No more feet on our necks, Babu.

Hasari backs off, leans against a wall, stares down at Ashoka, his hands in tight against his body. Manooj stares at his father in awe.
Shambu sees something on the ground where the first blow was delivered. His foot slides over and picks up Max's medallion and chain, raises it slowly to where his hand can grab it and stow it away.
The Goonda and thugs vanish, leaving Ashoka cowering in a doorway on his knees.
Max's gaze is on Hasari's face, then falls to take in his stomach wound, now pouring blood. He quickly gets Hasari to the rickshaw, instructs the kids to apply pressure, and takes off for the clinic as fast as he can pull.

[Max's room]
It is night. *The Raft of the Medusa* hangs on the wall. Hasari is in bed, with Kamla keeping vigil by his side. Max holds Shambu and Manooj close to him.

MAX
You gotta be brave, little fellas, 'cause your Daddy wants you to. See that picture, see those guys on the front looking off into the distance? Like you and your Baba, they're full of hope, but now see that guy on the back of the raft with his chin on his hand like you? Well, like the old Magic Max, he spends all his time being afraid, scared of all the bad things that can happen. But the guys on the front, they never give up. And you know

The Raft of the Medusa, *by Théodore Géricault. Courtesy Art Resource.*

The Raft of the Medusa

A reproduction of the famous nineteenth century French painting, *The Raft of the Medusa* by Géricault, hangs in Joan's room at the City of Joy clinic. To Roland Joffé the painting suggested a comparison between life in Calcutta and a shipwreck.

"The painting is linked in my mind with another image: playing on a seesaw in the playground when I was nine or ten. We went very fast, up and down, and the whole point is that you have to push back to get off the ground. A younger child nearby was having a bad time because he didn't know you had to push back or wasn't strong enough, so he got a hard whack each time. Seesawing to him was nothing more than a series of unpleasant, meaningless, jarring bumps. Not so for his companion on the other end, for whom it was a series of delightful leaps and descents.

"Art historians suggest that Géricault is dramatizing some survivors on the raft gesturing heroically toward a ship that may or may not be about to rescue them. They are at the top of the raft, uplifted. On the lower end, hidden by an enormous swell, is a group sunk in despair. Géricault seems to be asking us which is true, or more properly telling us that both are. In this moment, swept along by the forces of nature, we see mankind, puny yet magnificent, in perpetual balance between victory and defeat. An actual survivor of the *Medusa* shipwreck is quoted as saying, 'We were suspended between hope and fear.'

"Hope and optimism are magnificently creative. They may not be justified but they are deeply human emotions. The street clinics in Calcutta reminded me of the painting, of a shipwreck.

"The background for using it in the film was that Joan, on her way to India, goes to an antique shop looking for something to remind her of home and civilization. When the antique dealer finds out where she is going, he pulls out a reproduction of the *Raft* and says, 'You'll know why I've given you this after you've been there a while.' That's the story we developed for Pauline Collins in our actors' workshop."

what makes it possible to make it through all the rough stuff? Our love for each other.

Hasari turns his head towards Max and the boys.

MANOOJ AND SHAMBU
(running to sit on the bed)
Baba!

HASARI
Max Daddah . . . For a long time I wanted you to leave. You made me feel things I have never felt before. But I'm glad you came to my country. I will ask the gods to bless each day of your absence.

Sounds of rickshaw bells.

HASARI
What's that? Am I dream? Rickshaw bells.

Shambu looks out the window.

SHAMBU
Baba, Baba, look!

They all help Hasari to sit up and make his way to the window. Outside, rickshaw pullers fill the courtyard and spill out into the street. When the window opens, all the pullers again start ringing their bells, and the room is full of their music.

HASARI
(shaking his head)
When we came to the city, we knew no one. Now . . .
(he smiles)
If the journey isn't what you expect, don't be surprised. My father said that to me before we left the village.

He starts to cough and is helped back to the bed.

A worried Shambu leads Max back to the window. Max bends close.

SHAMBU
(whispering)
Is my father going to be dead?

MAX
Get serious. You're father's going to be fine.

SHAMBU
Does my father needs gold?

Max nods. Shambu slips a hand into his clothing and brings out the medallion.

SHAMBU
Is this a gold?

MAX
(his eyes widening)
Yes, that's gold.

Calcutta and the Color of Light

No one can be indifferent to Calcutta. Love it or hate it, it is a city that constantly assails your senses and pulls at your emotions. Director of Photography Peter Biziou, winner of an Academy Award for his work on *Mississippi Burning*, had the task of capturing this once golden but now decaying city on screen.

"To my eyes Calcutta is really attractive and interesting," says Biziou. "It's a dream for any cinematographer. The contrast between highlight and shadow is interesting to photograph. The water-stained, chipped walls of buildings formed the background, while the dominant colors were the costumes of the people. Fabrics are made with strong mineral or vegetable dyes, and people wash their clothes so many times that you get amazing, faded-out yet strong colors.

"People wonder if the harsh midday sun wasn't difficult with Eastern skin tones. But it wasn't really because with the pastel colors predominating, I could open up the exposure a little more and see into faces without letting anything over-expose."

Biziou does not believe in contrived lighting. He will remain true to the source of light, even if it is very low. "Generally I try not to use any lamps for lighting people's faces in daylight. It usually feels false and you often see spots in people's eyes. I will bank three or four 12-foot-square reflectors to reflect sunlight; it's a very soft effect, very natural and kind to everyone. I don't like to push light into people's faces against the sunlight."

Top: *Kamla's and Amrita's costumes display the vibrant yet soft colors so effective on film.* Above: *Roland Joffé, Camera Operator Mike Roberts, and Director of Photography Peter Biziou line up a shot on the remote camera.*

The amount and range of camera equipment carried by the *City of Joy* unit would not be considered unusual by any western film unit, but to the impoverished Bengali film industry it was extraordinary. Biziou had a variety of cameras, including a steadicam, a remotely controlled camera perched atop a crane, and a lightweight precision camera that could be mounted underneath a rickshaw for certain effects.

If Biziou appreciated the natural environment of Calcutta, the human elements often proved trying. Because of all the disruptions in shooting, "We will never know the film that might have been made, but we made a film with great heart and great energy."

Everything shall pass away—
Yet I love,
When in its joyous flow
The smile of existence gleams
In the midst of destruction.
From the *vina* of death
Pours forth the song of life,
Lovely in its restlessness.

from "The Evermoving,"
by Rabindranath Tagore

SHAMBU
Now my sister can get married?

MAX
Now your sister can get married . . . all because of you.

The boy's hopeful face finally breaks into a smile.

[The Pals' room]
We see the fully blossomed flower in the tea caddy, and
then Hasari's fingers come into the frame. He carefully
snips the flower free of its stalk.
    Amrita is dressed in the beautiful sari her father
bought her. Father and daughter are alone. He hands
her the flower and adjusts her veil tenderly.

"Our Sacred Duty and Honor"

The ancient Indian custom of the marriage dowry was officially abolished after the country won independence, but it still thrives. "The marriage of a daughter is a sacred duty for a father," Dominique Lapierre notes. "Once his last daughter had left home, the old man would have completed his task on earth. Then at last he would be able to await in peace the visitation of Yama, the god of the dead."

Not only must the bride's father often go into debt for a dowry, the cost of the marriage ceremony is his entire responsibility as well. Even very poor families somehow manage to provide elaborate feasts and clothe their daughter in an elegant wedding sari and because weddings traditionally take place at night, due to astrological considerations, illumination must be provided at extra cost.

"An Indian girl's dowry is made up of two parts," continues Lapierre. "One part consists of her trousseau and personal jewels. The other part of made up of the gifts she will take to her new family." In the case of Hasari's daughter, Amrita, "the list included two cotton saris, two bodices, a shawl, various household utensils, and a few imitation jewels and ornaments. It was true that it was a poor man's dowry, but it represented some two thousand rupees, a fabulous sum for a poverty-stricken rickshaw *wallah*."

Ironically, the dowry that may have led one family further down the spiral of poverty often serves as the new family's hedge against disaster—collateral they can use to borrow against in extra-lean times. Many in India

Amrita in her wedding sari.

today, however, call for doing away with the entire cycle; actress Shabana Azmi, who plays Hasari's wife Kamla, is active in the anti-dowry movement.

HASARI
This grew from a tiny seed. You never did belong to me. You were only lent to me by God until you marry and continue the wheel of life.

Amrita stares at her father and then kneels and lays her head in his lap. Tears fill Hasari's eyes, but a smile graces his lips.

[The square]
It is early evening of the wedding day. The procession to the courtyard begins when a band strikes up, accompanied by singing and shouting. Tiny lights have been strung over the street. We see Max with Joan and Poomina. Margareta and a group of children. Anouar, Meeta, Said. Everyone who's become part of this family is present.

The procession arrives and enters. Smoke from the *chulas*. Light from a half dozen lamps. Subash and his family make their entrance. A ritual veil is fixed to Subash's face. The *pujari* waves for Hasari to come to his place. Hasari turns to Max.

HASARI

I would be honored if you would come and sit next to my father—to bless the daughter.

Deeply touched, Max nods. The ceremony proceeds with the winding of the red thread. Hasari looks on with unspeakable pride.

Later, during the celebration, Joan and Max are sitting together watching.

JOAN

Well, Junior, I'll bet you never imagined you'd be giving away a daughter at your age, in the middle of a slum in Calcutta.

MAX

And I'll bet you never expected me to say I'm glad, no, I'm happy to be here. I mean, it may not look like you achieve anything when you drill a hole in water, but I realize it's sure as hell worth the effort, Sister Joan.

A pause. Their eyes connect.

JOAN

Now you're free to go.

The marriage ceremony: Amrita and Subash, center, with Subash's father and the Ghosh uncles behind them; Kamla and Hasari, right.

> In a traffic accident, Hasari Pal met a Bengali taxi driver who befriended him and gave him a ride in his taxi, an experience that instantly elevated Hasari's ambitions. "Instead of gripping the shafts of a rickshaw, his hands caressed a steering wheel; instead of treading asphalt and holes, his feet traveled deftly between three small rubber pedals; instead of straining and sweating, he earned his children's rice seated calmly on the seat of a chariot more noble than Arjuna's. A taxi! What rickshaw puller has not dreamed that one day the four arms of the god Viswakarma would gently touch his rattling cart and transform it into one of those black-and-yellow vehicles that streaked through the avenues of Calcutta."
>
> Dominique Lapierre,
> *The City of Joy*

MAX
No, now I'm free to stay.

JOAN
Well, maybe we'll find something for you to do.

They embrace.
Hasari beckons to Max. Max comes to him. Hasari is holding his side. He half lifts his hand from his wound; it's bleeding.

HASARI
No one must see. This is their time for happiness.

Hasari puts his hand on his friend's shoulder, and they walk through the crowd of wedding guests. Hasari, leaning lightly on Max, smiles right and left at well-wishers, concealing his pain. They walk up the lane together past the rickshaw, whose shafts point up at the vast sky. Max puts out his hand to steady his friend.

HASARI
I want to walk on my own, Max Daddah.

He grips Max's shoulder for a moment to show that no rejection is intended. They walk up the lane together. Max stops to check Hasari's bandage.

MAX
Okay, let's see.

HASARI
Is it bad?

MAX
Is it fatal? It will be if I can't keep you in bed for more than two minutes. You've got too much to do yet. You've got two sons to put through school, wives to find, a rickshaw to pull . . . maybe a taxi to drive.

HASARI
(smiles)
A taxi. You know, Max Daddah, the gods haven't made it easy to be a human being.

MAX
No, they haven't.
(a pause)
I guess that's why it feels so goddam wonderful to beat the odds.

Their hands come together, brown and white, bonded, bound. They walk off together down the lane.

And the wheel continues to turn. As Amrita and Subash, joined by the thread, circle the flame, we pull back and up to see the clinic and school and the surrounding area, the alleys full of people and activity.

As we continue to pull back, we see the entirety of the City of Joy and then beyond, Calcutta, its teeming streets, life continuing as the sun sets against an infinite sky.

"You are invited to the festival of this world and your life is blessed."

Rabindranath Tagore

CITY OF JOY

PATRICK SWAYZE as Max Lowe

PAULINE COLLINS as Joan Bethel

OM PURI as Hasari Pal

SHABANA AZMI as Kamla Pal

ART MALIK as Ashoka

AYESHA DHARKER as Amrita Pal

SANTU CHOWDHURY as Shambu Pal

IMRAN BADSAH KHAN as Manooj Pal

DEBTOSH GHOSH as Ram Chander

SUNEETA SENGUPTA as Poomina

MANSI UPADHYAY as Meeta

BAROON CHAKRABORTY as Said

SHYAMANAND JALAN as Mr. Ghatak

Directed by ROLAND JOFFÉ

Produced by JAKE EBERTS and ROLAND JOFFÉ

Co-Producer IAIN SMITH

Screenplay by MARK MEDOFF

Based on the book by DOMINIQUE LAPIERRE

Director of Photography PETER BIZIOU, B.S.C.

Production Designed by ROY WALKER

Film Editor GERRY HAMBLING, A.C.E.

Costume Designer JUDY MOORCROFT

Casting by PRISCILLA JOHN

Music Composed, Orchestrated, and Conducted by
ENNIO MORRICONE

A LIGHTMOTIVE PRODUCTION
A ROLAND JOFFÉ FILM

A Tristar Pictures Release, U.S. and Canada
Allied Filmmakers, N.V. and Warner Bros. International, all other countries

✤ My Love Story with the City of Joy ✤

by Dominique Lapierre

Dominique Lapierre has donated half his royalties to support schools, dispensaries, and homes for the leper children of Calcutta. He is seen here with his wife, also called Dominique, and some of their young protégés. Photo by Dominique Conchon.

That very first monsoon morning when I walked into it, I knew that this wretched slum of Calcutta called the City of Joy was one of the most extraordinary places on our planet. I left it two years later with some twenty pads full of notes and hundreds of hours of tape. They contained, I knew, the material for the greatest book of my career, an epic of heroism, love, and faith, a glorious tribute to the human ability to overcome adversity, to survive every possible tragedy.

During that long, difficult, and sometimes painful research, I learned how people could live with rats, scorpions, and insects, survive on a few spoonfuls of rice and one or two bananas a day, queue up for hours for latrines, wash with less than a pint of water, light a match in the monsoon, share their living quarters with a group of eunuchs. Before being adopted by the inhabitants of the slum, I had to learn their customs, experience their fears and their misery, share their struggles and their hopes. It was one of the most extraordinary experiences a writer could live. It changed my life.

Living with the heroic inhabitants of the City of Joy transformed my sense of priorities and of the true values of life. After this confrontation with the real issues of existence—hunger, disease, total absence of medical facilities, lack of work—I no longer fight for things like a parking place when I return to Europe or America. Sharing for all those months the lives of a population who might have as little as the equivalent of twenty-five cents per day with which to survive taught me the real value of things. Now I instinctively turn off the electricity when I leave a room, use my bar of soap to the very end, avoid throwing into the garbage can what can be saved or used again. These unique experiences taught me something else— the beauty of sharing with others. For two years nothing was

asked of me but much was given. The generosity of my friends in the City of Joy showed me that true meaning of the beautiful Indian proverb that says: "All that is not given is lost."

It took me one full year to write the epic of *The City of Joy*. I wrote the book in my home in the South of France, in the beautiful and privileged privacy of Provence's pine woods and vineyards. To remind me constantly of the anthill of Calcutta—its noises, it smells, it colors—every day before I began writing, I first looked at a few of the two thousand photographs I had taken and ran some of the tapes of local life I had recorded.

The final version of *The City of Joy* was first published in France, then in Spain, Italy, Holland, Germany, England, and the United States. Everywhere its success was immediate, enormous, and for me totally unexpected in its dimension. The book has now sold more than six million copies in thirty-one languages and editions, including five editions in Braille for the blind.

Although I was convinced that I had written an inspiring saga, I was truly surprised by the success that the story of a Calcutta slum enjoyed. Even more surprising was the mail that began to pour into my Paris apartment. Thousands of readers from all over the world sent me letters, each an homage of gratitude to *The City of Joy*. In almost every one of the envelopes was a check, sometimes a small package with a piece of jewelry,

Dominique Lapierre has been visiting Calcutta for forty years. He and his wife return to the streets of the city several times a year to work on their humanitarian projects. Photo by Baldev/Sygma.

a gold ingot, or a stack of stock exchange shares. One letter contained a short, anonymous message saying: *"The City of Joy is so beautiful that we are happy to send the enclosed items. Please sell them. They will be more useful in the City of Joy than around our fingers."* Taped to the sheet of paper were two wedding rings.

One day, as I was leaving my apartment to rush to Charles de Gaulle airport for a flight to New York, the doorbell rang. At the door was an old woman with a travel bag. "I have just arrived by train from Toulouse," she announced. "I have come here to write my will in favor of your heroes of the City of Joy." The story of these heroes has touched so many hearts that school children have organized collections in their classes, and produced plays and shows on their behalf. Hundreds of readers have offered to adopt a child from the City of Joy, or to devote their next vacation to going there to help.

On my side, I have offered half of all my royalties to the heroes of my book or to humanitarian institutions in Calcutta and its vicinity struggling to improve the lives of the poorest of the poor. Since the book was first published in 1985, almost two million dollars have been sent from my royalties and from donations of readers to create, support, and develop a whole series of top-priority projects. These include refuge centers for lepers and polio children, dispensaries, schools, rehabilitation workshops, education programs, sanitary actions, and so forth. To process and channel the funds, I have founded an association called "Action Aid for Lepers' Children of Calcutta," which now has several thousand members. Its headquarters are located at 26 Avenue Kléber, 75116 Paris, France. Readers are invited to join us to help support new projects.

One afternoon in December 1987, the mayor of Calcutta, Mr. K. K. Basu, and his whole Municipal Council, gave my wife and me a splendid reception at the City Hall to express the city's gratitude for the way I had "told the world about the virtues of courage, vitality, and hope of its population." On this occasion we were made citizens of honor of the metropolis and given its gold medal of honor.

But the most surprising and significant award I was to receive on that memorable day was an impressive document showing the impact my book had on the administrators of the city. It was the plans for a municipal development project called "Calcutta—City of Joy—Designs for Tomorrow." Among the very first actions outlined by this document to change life conditions in the city and make it a real "city of joy" was to supply the three million slum residents with ten liters per capita of drinkable water each day.

Every day I spent with the inhabitants of the City of Joy, I thought of the fantastic film their story could make. I felt that such a tale of courage, of love, of vitality and hope would be an inspiration for every human being on this planet. It was an adventure in survival, a reason to believe in man's eternal capacity to be bigger than adversity.

Late in 1985, the great British director Roland Joffé and the Canadian producer Jake Eberts came to see me in Paris to express their interest in bringing my book to the screen. Joffé had directed two of my favorite films, *The Killing Fields* and *The Mission*, and Eberts had been involved in the production of *Gandhi*, a magnificent cinematic tribute to the father of modern India, inspired among other sources by *Freedom at Midnight*, the book I had coauthored with Larry Collins about India's struggle for independence. Joffé was exactly the man to give an epic dimension to the saga I had written.

He wanted to film the story exactly where it took place, in the very anthill of Calcutta, with the people of the city as protagonists. This was a fantastic idea but, in my opinion, totally unrealistic. I knew from experience that if you walked in a street of Calcutta taking photos with a pocket camera, you were immediately surrounded by twenty people. If you had in your hand an amateur video camera, the number would jump to fifty or a hundred. What would happen when trucks with filming equipment, lights, cranes, dollies, suddenly appeared in the boiling cauldron of that unpredictable city? Joffé was sure that he could handle the problem. He felt that the film absolutely had to capture the unique atmosphere of this unique place. It was, we both realized, an extraordinary challenge, probably the boldest cinematic adventure ever undertaken.

As we talked in my Paris apartment, full of Indian memorabilia, I could visualize the glorious faces of all my friends in Calcutta, those men, women, and children whom I had called "the lights of the world." I had tried to be their voice. I felt proud that a leading film director now wanted to tell their story on the screen. I agreed to the project, and Joffé assigned the scriptwriting to Mark Medoff, the brilliant and compassionate author of *Children of a Lesser God.*

One evening in October 1989, as I lay in a hospital bed in Toulouse recovering from an operation that was to cure me of cancer, I received a phone call from Calcutta. Joffé wanted to know if I would be upset if they changed Stephan Kovalski, the Polish priest in the book, into a woman, in order to avoid an all-male cast in the lead roles. I agreed instantly: for me, what counted was that the film translate the spirit of the book to the screen, not the sex of its characters!

Along streets of Calcutta's urban village. Director ...

City of Protests

An Author and Ronald Joffe

the madness.
"Roll 'em"
"Action!"

High Court order on City of Joy

a jostling

'City of
wood to
arges

...rmined to
...inue filmi...

LF plans rallies City of Joy

By Our Special Re...

made life impossi-

By Our Legal Reporter

M...R Justice N. K. Mitra of Ca...
...cutta High Court on Thurs...
day directed the City of Joy film
makers to restrict the shooting
indoors at the Paharpur sets
the land of the ...

"City" of Controversy

In September 1990, five years after Roland Joffé and producer Jake Eberts had purchased the rights to *City of Joy*, the cameras began to roll in Calcutta. But shooting on the city's streets proved to be fraught with problems. Aware of its shortcomings and proud of its achievements, Calcuttan officials and intellectuals were concerned that this group of Westerners would produce an overly negative picture of their city.

The Marxist West Bengal state government had already decided that Dominique Lapierre's book was inaccurate and exploitive, a reversal of position after having feted and honored the author on its publication. To many of the critics, it did not matter that the film was a loose adaptation of certain elements in the book, not a literal translation to the screen.

The filmmakers did their best to cooperate, with co-producer Iain Smith as the primary contact between the crew and the government, press, and street demonstrators. A respected local author was brought in to vet the script and ensure its strand of authenticity, but this did not still the opposition. Various officials and newspapers

continued to campaign against the film from the first to last day of shooting. Paid demonstrators invaded the set, firebombs were thrown, and a series of injunctions lodged in local court to disrupt the filmmaking. All this took its toll on the budget, the choice of locations, and the actors' concentration.

"Making *City of Joy* was never going to be an easy enterprise," says Joffé. "I knew we would touch certain nerves in Calcutta, and it would be difficult to control the tremor. Every film made in India has experienced the same problems, especially in Calcutta. At the same time, there is a warmth, a sense of humor and humanity there, and I hoped if we kept these things on our side, we would be okay.

"Some of our difficulties stemmed from the very different ways in which Westerners and Indians regard 'truth.' To us it's an objective reality: as when members of our crew were accused of attacking a reporter during a demonstration. Clearly they did not, and his death was proved to be from natural causes. But to the paper's editor, who wanted me to fire the crew members, truth was a matter of perception and saving face. If I wouldn't help him, why should he help me?"

The filmmakers did not ask for unqualified acceptance, but for the freedom to make a film that would be judged as a complete work. To deny this was to compromise the basic right of any artist to work without censorship or interference. Joffé also argued—in one case in the middle of a demonstration— that preventing the Indian actors from working was an injustice to them; they deserved their turn on the world's stage.

"I would have liked some discussion, which would have eased the minds of a lot of people who were worried. They would have realized that this was not a film selling poverty or the shock value of Calcutta. It is a story about the inordinate power that resides in the human spirit." Nevertheless, he believes, "compared to what goes on in Calcutta every day, we were getting off pretty lightly. Ninety percent of the people were with us."

Iain Smith adds, "We were privileged to have seen this city as most foreigners never get to see it—not all bad and not all good. Calcutta is a little like my native Glasgow, wanting desperately to be loved but often provoking the opposite."

The shooting of *City of Joy* began on February 9, 1991. As I had feared, the descent of such an important foreign production on the streets of my beloved but volatile Calcutta could not go unnoticed. A handful of politicians and professional agitators, more eager to get their names in the newspapers than to improve their fellow citizens' living conditions, soon began a crusade against the filmmaking. Copies of the script found their way to scandal magazines, which hastened to publish, out of context, the scenes involving lepers or mafia activities, in order to fuel the notion that India's poverty was being exploited by Hollywood.

Some of the agitators turned on me as, in March 1991, I was visiting the humanitarian centers of Bengal sponsored with my royalties. One night the French Consul General called to urge my wife and me to move quickly out of our residence. The chief of police had just informed him that a big demonstration was going to take place the next morning in front of our guest house, and that "things might get nasty." Newspapers and magazines faked interviews in which I was supposed to have accused Roland Joffé of "completely twisting the spirit" of my book. Booksellers were warned that their shops would be looted and burned if they continued to sell copies of *The City of Joy*. By that time, the book had become so popular that three pirate editions in Bengali were sold by hawkers on the sidewalks of the city.

Joffé, his producers, his actors, and his crew proved stronger than all adversities. Inspired themselves by the courage and resilience of the characters they were portraying, they managed to overcome all obstacles.

One morning in late March, as the controversy and political agitation raged against their enterprise, my wife and I were invited to a small ceremony in the slum where it all began, organized by a group of its residents. As we walked into the area, I was surprised to discover a huge banner hanging across one of the main alleys: "DOMINIQUE LAPIERRE—WELCOME HOME— THE CITY OF JOY."

From the waiting crowd ran a young girl with a bouquet of flowers. I recognized my old friend Padmini, the heroic little Bengali girl who used to get up every morning at four and go out on the railway embankment to pick up burning pieces of coal that had fallen from the locomotives—a miserable treasure, the sale of which helped her family survive day after day. Padmini was beaming. "Take these flowers, Dominique *Daddah* (big brother)," she said. "Because, thanks to your book and Mr. Joffé's film, we will no more be alone in our City of Joy."

❖ FOR FURTHER READING ❖

The following titles were among the sources used in the preparation of the film and this book; they will provide readers with a wealth of background information about Calcutta and India.

Bhattacharya, Deben, trans. *Songs of the Bards of Bengal.* New York: Grove Press, Inc., 1969. Translations of the oral verse of the Baul poets, wandering poet-troubadours who traverse rural Bengal. The songs are religious, meant to impart teachings from master to disciple.

Bose, Aurobindo, trans. *Later Poems of Rabindranath Tagore.* New York: Funk & Wagnalls, 1976. A Bengal native, Tagore won the Nobel Prize for Literature in 1913 and is India's most revered literary figure.

Brata, Sasthi. *India: Labyrinths in the Lotus Land.* New York: William Morrow and Co., 1985. A writer and journalist based in London combines personal observation and history of his native land.

Collins, Larry and Dominique Lapierre. *Freedom at Midnight.* New York: Avon Books, 1976. Lapierre and co-author Collins dramatize the sweeping events that led to India's independence after three centuries of British rule.

Grass, Günter. *Show Your Tongue.* New York: Harcourt Brace Jovanovich, Inc., 1989. A controversial, often negative portrait of Calcutta by the contemporary German novelist.

Lapierre, Dominique. *The City of Joy: An Epic of Love, Heroism, and Hope in the India of Mother Teresa.* New York: Warner Books, 1992. Lapierre's vast portrait of life in the bustees of Calcutta encompasses rickshaw pullers, religious festivals, the dedicated people who work to aid "the poorest of the poor," and much more.

Mehta, Ved. *Portrait of India.* New York: Farrar, Straus & Giroux, 1967. A selective history and travelogue about India by an expatriate Indian writer.

Meigh, Frances. *Destitutes of Calcutta: The Jack Preger Story.* Cornwall, England: Tabb House, 1988. A profile of Dr. Jack and his work by an English-woman who worked with him in Calcutta.

Moorhouse, Geoffrey. *Calcutta.* New York: Harcourt Brace Jovanovich, Inc., 1971. A wide-ranging and incisive biography of Calcutta by a British journalist.

Muggeridge, Malcolm. *Something Beautiful for God: Mother Teresa of Calcutta.* New York: Harper & Row, 1986. This account is based on interviews conducted by the author with Mother Teresa for a BBC television film of the same name.

Naipaul, V. S. *An Area of Darkness.* New York: Viking Penguin, 1992. A sharp-edged view of India by the noted author.

Prabhavananda, Swami and Christopher Isherwood, trans. *Bhagavad-Gita: The Song of God.* Hollywood: Vedanta Press, 1965. One of India's great sacred texts, taking the form of a dialogue between the warrior-prince Arjuna and the god Krishna.

❖ Acknowledgments ❖

Permission to reprint copyrighted material from the following sources is gratefully acknowledged.

An Area of Darkness by V.S. Naipaul. Copyright © 1964 by V.S. Naipaul. Used by permission of Vintage Books, Random House, Inc.

Bathing in the Hooghly River, photograph by Johnston and Hoffman. Reprinted by permission from *The Last Empire: Photography in British India, 1855-1911*, Aperture, 1976.

Bhagavad-Gita: The Song of God, translated by Swami Prabhavananda and Christopher Isherwood. Copyright © 1944, 1951 by the Vedanta Society of Southern California. Used by permission of the Vedanta Society.

Calcutta by Geoffrey Moorhouse. Copyright © 1971 by Geoffrey Moorhouse. Used by permission of the author.

The Calcutta Psyche. India International Centre Quarterly (Vol. 17, Nos. 3-4). Copyright © 1990 India International Centre. Used by permission.

The City of Joy by Dominique Lapierre. Copyright © 1985 by Dominique Lapierre; English translation copyright © 1985 by Pressinter, S.A. Used by permission of Warner Books and Dominique Lapierre.

Destitutes of Calcutta: The Jack Preger Story by Frances Meigh. Copyright © 1988 by Frances Meigh. Used by permission of Tabb House.

Dr. Jack Preger, photograph by Allen Jewhurst. Used by courtesy of Chameleon Films and by permission of the photographer.

Drawings by Imtiaz Dharker. Used by permission of the artist.

India: Labyrinths in the Lotus Land by Sasthi Brata. Copyright © 1985 by Sasthi Brata. Used by permission of William Morrow and Company, Inc.

Kalighat Paintings. A catalog and introduction by W. G. Archer. Copyright © 1971 by Her Majesty's Stationery Office. By courtesy of the Board of Trustees of the Victoria & Albert Museum.

Khajuraho Bullocks and *Movie Billboards*, photographs by Robert Holmes. Copyright © 1988 by Robert Holmes. Used by permission of the photographer.

Later Poems of Rabindranath Tagore, translated by Aurobindo Bose. Copyright © 1974 by Peter Owen Ltd. Translation copyright © 1974 by Aurobindo Bose. Used by permission of Peter Owen Publishers.

Mother Teresa, photograph by Symil Kumar Dutt/Camera Press London.

Portrait of India by Ved Mehta. Copyright © 1967, 1968, 1969, 1970 by Ved Mehta. Used by permission of Farrar, Straus and Giroux.

Raft of the Medusa, painting by Théodore Géricault. Used by permission of Scala/Art Resource, New York; Louvre, Paris.

Satyajit Ray, photograph by Sunil Janah. Used by permission of the photographer.

Something Beautiful for God: Mother Teresa of Calcutta by Malcolm Muggeridge. Copyright © 1971 by The Mother Teresa Committee. Used by permission of HarperCollins, and William Collins Sons & Co. Ltd.

Songs of the Bards of Bengal, translated by Deben Bhattacharya. Copyright © 1969 by UNESCO. Used by permission of Grove Press, Inc.

The excerpts from Dominique Lapierre's *The City of Joy* used in this book represent only a small selection from the original source.

The publisher wishes to thank the following for their special contributions: Robin Chaykin of Lightmotive, Ltd., who followed up on countless details with great efficiency and good humor; Ben Myron of Lightmotive, Tristan Whalley of Majestic Films, Irene Lyons of Katevale, Kate Arbeid and John Trehy of the *City of Joy* production staff, and Barbara Lakin of TriStar Pictures for their expedient support and cooperation; the staffs of Walking Stick Press and Newmarket Press for their unflagging commitment to excellence despite scheduling and communications challenges; Patrick Swayze for his inspiring work in this film and instant encouragement of our book project; Iain Smith and Priscilla John for sharing their experience on the film's production; and Ann Tasker for her wonderfully detailed production notes. We owe special thanks to Mark Medoff for his affecting screenplay and original contribution to this book; to Dominique Lapierre, for his enlightening afterword, contribution of his own photographs, and generous permission for the use of excerpts from his extraordinary original work, and his wife, Dominique Conchon-Lapierre, for her help in researching photos, writing captions, and answering queries. And above all, to Roland Joffé and Jake Eberts, for writing out their fascinating personal reflections and supporting so enthusiastically and productively the making of this book about their wonderful film.

❖ About the Authors ❖

Roland Joffé directs his fourth film with *City of Joy*. His first, *The Killing Fields*, won three Academy Awards and seven British Academy Awards (the latter including Best Picture). It also won Italy's Michelangelo Prize and was nominated for a Cesar in France. *The Mission*, starring Robert De Niro and Jeremy Irons, won Oscars for cinematography and original music, the Palme d'Or at Cannes, and other international honors. In 1989 he completed *Fat Man and Little Boy*, the compelling drama of the development of the atomic bomb.

Joffé was born in London and studied English and drama at Manchester University. After graduating, he went to work as one of the founding directors of the Young Vic Theatre and next joined Britain's National Theatre Company, then under the direction of Laurence Olivier. Joffé then moved into television, directing local news, soap operas, current affairs programs, documentary films, and dramatic series. His television work has also earned many awards.

Joffé is a founding member of the Cambodia Trust, which raises money for health and education for Cambodian war victims. He is also a member of Survival International, which works to protect indigenous tribal populations in many countries.

Jake Eberts has been associated with the production of some of the most distinguished and successful films of recent times. As founder and chief executive of Goldcrest Films from 1977 to 1984, he helped to finance, produce, or distribute *Gandhi*, *The Killing Fields*, *Escape from New York*, *The Howling*, *Chariots of Fire*, *Local Hero*, and *The Dresser*. Goldcrest also developed the television miniseries *Robin Hood*, *The Far Pavilions*, and Emmy Award winner *Concealed Enemies*.

In 1984 Eberts joined Embassy Films, where his first task was raising funds for and overseeing John Boorman's *The Emerald Forest*. In 1986, he founded Allied Filmmakers, which has arranged or provided funding for fifteen feature films including

Name of the Rose, Hope & Glory, Driving Miss Daisy, and *Dances With Wolves.*

Born in Montreal and educated at McGill University, Eberts worked on Wall Street and in the London financial community before entering the film industry.

MARK MEDOFF, who authored the screenplay for *City of Joy*, won a Tony Award for his 1980 play, *Children of a Lesser God.* He was nominated for an Academy Award for the filmscript of *Children* and an ACE award for his HBO Premiere movie, *Apology.* He won an Obie Award for his 1973 play, *When You Comin Back, Red Ryder. Children, Red Ryder,* and *The Wager* were included in Ten Best Plays for their New York seasons.

Medoff holds degrees from the University of Miami (B.A.), Stanford University (M.A.), and an honorary Doctor of Humane Letters from Gallaudet University. He is Dramatist in Residence and Professor of Theatre Arts at New Mexico State University, where he has been on the faculty for twenty-six years. He was Head of Theatre Arts for nine years and Artistic Director of the American Southwest Theatre Company for five years.

His novel, *Dreams of Long Lasting,* will be published by Warner Books in June 1992. Medoff lives in Las Cruces, New Mexico, with his wife, Stephanie, and two of his three daughters.

DOMINIQUE LAPIERRE has been producing bestselling books since 1948, when he wrote *A Dollar for A Thousand Miles,* based on his experiences working his way across the Atlantic on a ship and touring North America on a shoestring. The following year he returned to America, where he met and married his wife, also named Dominique, then a fashion magazine editor. His second book was based on their round-the-world honeymoon.

In the 1950s, Lapierre became an international correspondent for *Paris Match* and was the first Western journalist granted permission to travel through post-Stalin Soviet Russia in his own car, resulting in another bestseller. In 1960, he began his extraordinarily successful partnership with the American writer Larry Collins; their books include the World War II classic *Is Paris Burning?; . . . Or I'll Dress You in Mourning,* a panorama of the Spanish Civil War; *O Jerusalem* and *Freedom at Midnight,* their epics about the birth of the modern states of Israel and India, respectively; and the 1980 novel *The Fifth Horseman.*

Writing solo, Lapierre's most recent works are *The City of Joy,* which has sold more than six and a half million copies in thirty-one countries and languages, and *Beyond Love,* which reconstructs as a medical thriller the discovery of and battle against the AIDS virus.

The City of Joy has evoked the greatest popular response of all Lapierre's works. The author donates half his royalties from the book to support a number of humanitarian projects in India. The book won the prestigious American literary prize, the Christopher Award, whose motto is "Rather light a candle than curse the darkness."